Identity Theft

Protecting yourself when the enemy strikes

KAREN POWERS
FOREWORD BY ELMER TOWNS

21stCENTURY
P R E S S
READING YOU LOUD AND CLEAR.

IDENTITY THEFT

Copyright © 2011 by Karen Powers
Published by 21st Century Press
Springfield, Missouri U.S.A.
Printed in U.S.A.

21st Century Press is an evangelical Christian publisher dedicated to serving the local church with purpose books. We believe God's vision for 21st Century Press is to provide church leaders with biblical, user-friendly materials that will help them evangelize, disciple and minister to children, youth and families.

It is our prayer that this book will help you discover biblical truth for your own life and help you meet the needs of others. May God richly bless you.

21st Century Press
2131 W. Republic Rd. PMB 41
Springfield, MO 65807
800-658-0284
www.21stcenturypress.com

ISBN: 978-0-9838359-1-2
Cover: Hugo Calderon
Book Design: Lee Fredrickson

ACKNOWLEDGMENTS

There is no greater praise than what I can give to our Lord Jesus Christ. Thank you, Lord, for loving me so deeply, forgiving me so freely, instructing me so wisely, and sending me on the most incredible journey of a lifetime.

Thank you, Kent and Carol Siefker (dad and mom) for bringing Michael and I up in a Christian home and for providing for us, even when money was tight. Your encouragement has spurred us on to reach further and higher than we ever thought possible.

Thank you, Wendell, my husband, for loving me and listening to everything I have to say. You are the best sounding board that anyone could ever have. I cherish your "precious" family and your "priceless" Grammy.

Thank you, Laura, Ryan, and Lindsey for giving me a name to be treasured—MOM. You have taught me a lot about myself and have given me much joy. I am so proud of all of you. Always remember that my deepest wish for you is that you "Serve God with your whole heart—for your whole life."

Thank you, Cielo Vista Church, for giving me a rock-solid foundation. As a little girl, sitting under the leadership of Pastor John R. Morgan, to my life today serving in the ladies ministry and alongside my husband (the Student Pastor), I have been blessed beyond measure. Our lead pastor, Rod Smith, is humbly leading our church to fulfill the commission of Christ. Cielo Vista, you truly help people to Walk to Jesus, Walk with Jesus, and Walk like Jesus.

Thank you, Immanuel Christian School, for the privilege to teach your students over the past eleven years. And thank you, administration and staff, for pouring your hearts into my own three children. There is absolutely no doubt that you are the best Christian School in the region.

Thank you to all my dear friends and teachers over the years. God has blessed me so much by placing each of you in my life. Words will never be able to convey the thankfulness I feel to have been a part of your lives.

Thank you, Lee Fredrickson, for "Reading ME loud and clear." May our efforts together result in lives that are sold out to reaching the lost world and to building strong identities in Christ.

The author can be reached at:

Karen Powers, c/o Cielo Vista Church, 3585 N. Lee Trevino Dr., El Paso, TX 79936, or you may email: <u>karenpowers@cielovista.org</u>.

TABLE OF CONTENTS

FOREWORD

One of the most important items we have is our identity. When that is lost, life is lost.

Identity Theft tells you what to do when your spiritual identity is stolen. Thank God that a Christian is dealing with this issue in an intelligent yet biblical way.

As a pastor and minister for Christ, I have dealt with people whose minds have been "stolen" and they no longer have a self identity. Years ago I dealt with a young girl who had been given an overdose of drugs by several young men, and her mind was "burned out." I felt a sense of rage toward those young men that fed this young girl drugs that stole her mind.

And then I had been to nursing homes and other places to see those whose self identity is stolen by Alzheimer's or dementia; that also is a terrible state. I once talked to a man who had two doctoral degrees, one from Harvard University and the other from Princeton University, yet Alzheimer's had stolen his life, his self perception; his memory was gone. I thought what a terrible waste; he spent his life preparing to serve others, and then Alzheimer's stole everything from him.

Let's remember that the Bible teaches that we have an enemy who is satan or the devil. He is a thief and wants to steal everything from us. He will take away our victory, he will steal our reputation, and of course when all else fails, he will use Alzheimer's to steal a mind, or use some other physiological disorder to steal one's self identity and even their consciences.

In this book, Karen Powers writes about the dangers of modern day "spiritual" identity theft; whether by satan or those inspired by him. I am glad that Karen Powers has suggested ways to protect ourselves spiritually so we can live with a confident identity in Christ. May we all read and be wiser as we encounter this book.
—Elmer Towns
Author, Co-Founder, Liberty University
Dean, Liberty University School of Religion,
Liberty Baptist Theological Seminary and Graduate School

INTRODUCTION

Your identity... It's who you are. It's *everything* that you are. When you were born, you had a hospital bracelet clamped around your wrist to prove you were YOU. It's that identity that has stayed with you until now. You're still that same person. Or are you?

Satan wants you to believe that newborn life of long ago is worthless now. In fact, he is so engaged in your identity that he is doing everything in his power to take it away from you. But as a believer, you have all the power you need over him. You don't have to believe his lies about you. You can choose to deny those lies and claim your life back through the awesome power of Jesus Christ. Identity theft is no new phenomenon. The need for identity protection increases each day. God in His infinite wisdom saw ahead to this day and time of ever increasing technology and by "*His divine power has given us everything we need for life and godliness*" according to 2 Peter 1:3. Our problem is that we let Satan take our God given identity and power away from us.

It's time to claim that identity back. We *can't* let Satan get the victory here! As long as we live a life with even a speck of defeat, he HAS won. He's taken that victory from us. Just remember the last page of Satan's story. He LOSES in the end! And he knows it! Because WE are the victors, we need to claim our identity and live the abundant life that God intends for us to have. We must live victoriously. We must not let our sinful failures crowd out the joy and flowing forgiveness of God. We must live our lives with a confident identity in Him.

—Karen Powers

Chapter 1

IDENTITY THEFT

"But you are a chosen people, a royal priesthood, a holy nation, a people belonging to God, that you may declare the praises of Him who called you out of darkness into His wonderful light" (1 Peter 2:9).

Identity theft… In this age of technology that we are living in, almost everyone who hears those two words knows what they mean. It's when our physical, social, and financial information falls into the hands of a predator, who will take it and use it for his personal gain. In a society that is so computer savvy, serious identity protection is a must for everyone. Just knowing that everything that I have worked hard for on this earth could be lost in seconds leaves a hint of fear in the back of my mind. I know God doesn't want us to fear, but when more and more stories come out about the financial devastation caused by identity theft, I find myself saying an extra prayer or two over my possessions and their safety. Take the following scenario that is becoming a common occurrence at the checkout counter and see how a life can be changed from one moment to the next.

Marie unloaded her ten items onto the conveyor belt and watched her purchases topple toward the cashier. She hoped she hadn't forgotten anything. It always seemed that the instant she stepped away from the check out line she would remember that one missing item that she had come for in the first place.

With mind still wondering if she had forgotten anything, she reached for her debit card and swiped it through the machine. As she waited several moments for the next prompt, worry began to nag at her.

"What is taking so long?" she puzzled. "Is your machine working today?" she asked the cashier.

But the cashier was just as bewildered as she was. Marie's jaw dropped as the register message came up "denied."

Instant fear rushed her home to check on her online account. She knew she had plenty of money in her account. So what was the problem? As her accounts came up on the screen, she could see that charge after charge was listed on her bank account and credit card. While her bank account had plummeted, her credit card had skyrocketed. What she had always protected—her good credit—was now a just a wish and a prayer. Marie's good name was now red flagged. Apparently, she was the newest victim of identity theft.

That's right. Account overdrawn...credit card denied...unknown charges...identity theft...these are phrases that cause instant panic in us today. As much as we try to protect ourselves, we always wonder if we've done enough. Like Marie in the preceding story, we live in fear that at some point and at some time in our lives the words "identity theft" will become extremely personal and will echo in our own ears.

Why do we fear this? Well, it's perfectly normal to have these kinds of feelings. Television commercials and financial institutions are constantly warning us of the dangers out there. So we spend our lives trying to protect our basic freedoms and the possessions we have obtained because we know that in a brief second it can all be taken away from us. Our identity is a very personal thing, and if it's tampered with, we can feel violated and exposed.

As I was walking through the outlet mall near our city, I was reminded of how easily a person's identity could be taken away from them. On a bench out in the open sat a lady who was talking quite loudly on her cell phone. As I listened (because everyone who was within twenty yards could hear) she began to give her credit card number to the person she was talking to. I couldn't believe it! She was out in the middle of a public place and was freely divulging her private information. What was done was done—she couldn't take back the number that she had so loudly announced just minutes before, so I privately wished for her sake that nothing harmful would come of it.

As I thought about the naivety that had just taken place, I couldn't help but relate it to our spiritual walk. How many times do we, out of naivety, set ourselves up for an attack from Satan? We aren't informed with the Word and we fail to ask God for guidance, consequently, we end up succumbing to the cleverly crafted temptations of the devil. Just as the lady at the outlet mall was unaware of the danger she was putting herself in, we, too, can be unaware of the dangers we walk straight into when we don't consciously cover our lives with the blanket of protection that a committed life to Christ affords us.

Let's take a step back for a minute to digest this. Think about it—your identity—It's who you are. It's *everything* that you are. When you were born, you had a hospital bracelet clamped around your wrist to prove you were YOU. When you started kindergarten, you learned how to write that identity on the top of your paper in neat block letters. It's that same identity that is still with you today. You're still that same person. Or are you? In the twenty-first century, our identity is connected to more than just a name. It's also connected to every single thing that we own—from our bank account to our automobiles.

Satan is definitely not a fool when it comes to our spiritual identity. He knows how important our identity is to us and how lost and useless we feel when our identity is taken away. So guess what? He is going to try to sabotage everything we hold precious. If he can get you to believe that you are a failure and that you have become insignificant, then he has succeeded. He wants you to believe that precious newborn life of long ago is worthless now in today's world. In fact, he is so engaged in your identity that he is doing everything in his power to take it away from you. But as a believer, you have all the power you need over him. You don't have to believe his lies about you. You can choose to deny those lies and claim your life back through the awesome power of Jesus Christ.

Spiritual identity theft is no new phenomenon. God in His infinite wisdom saw ahead to this day and time and by "His divine power has given us everything we need for life and godliness" according to 2 Peter 1:3. John MacArthur, in *The MacArthur Bible Commentary*, explains it this way. "To be godly is to live reverently, loyally, and obediently toward God. Peter means that the genuine believer ought not to ask God for something more (as if something necessary to sustain his growth, strength, and perseverance was missing) to become godly, because he already has every spiritual resource to manifest, sustain, and perfect godly living." Even though we are fully equipped through Christ and have been given everything that we need as Christians, the problem we struggle with is that we allow Satan to take this power and God-given identity away from us. Instead of trying to combat Satan's attempt with God's power and the tools that He has given us to succeed in life, we end up trying to live our lives and serve God on our own.

But now it's time to claim that identity back. We *can't* let Satan get the victory here! As long as we live a life with even a speck of defeat, he has won. He's taken that victory from us. Just remember the last page of Satan's story. He's the one that loses in the end! And he knows it! Because WE are the victors, we need to claim our God-given identity and live the abundant life that God intends for us to have. We must live victoriously. We must not let our sinful failures crowd out the joy and flowing forgiveness of God. We must live our lives with a confident identity in Him.

It's interesting to see how many Bible characters had issues with their personal identities as well. Moses struggled with his identity and God gave him the select assignment to lead the Children of Israel out of Egypt. Notice that Exodus 3:11 says, *"But Moses said to God, 'Who am I, that I should go to Pharaoh and bring the Israelites out of Egypt?'"* King David realized his own insignificance when he said, *"O Lord, what is man that you care for him, the son of man that you think of him? Man is like a breath; his days are like a fleeting shadow"* (Psalm 144:3). Even the Apostle Paul had to face the demons of his past as he lived out his new found faith in front of the doubting disciples in Damascus and Jerusalem (Acts 9:19-27). The point is—we all struggle with our identity. Because our identities take root in our souls, our feelings and fears about them run deep. The comforting fact is that we are not alone in our quest to find out and preserve who we are. It is an innate desire, perhaps even a need, of most people today.

So come take a journey with me to find out who we really are—not who the world want us to be and certainly not who Satan wants us to be. We need to find out who God wants us to be. As we begin this journey together, it's important for us to watch out for public enemy number one—Satan. Once we've figured out his tricks, then we're on the road to discovering an identity that is fully protected.

Chapter 2

Just Who Does Satan Think He Is?

"Be sober, be vigilant; because your adversary the devil walks about like a roaring lion, seeking whom he may devour" (1 Peter 5:8 NKJV).

As a young girl, I was terrified of the devil. The church where I grew up did a tremendous job of teaching us that he was a dangerous creature and should be avoided at all cost. They also did a phenomenal job of teaching who God was, but in my young and imaginative mind, I became petrified of the devil. My fears outranked my capacity to reason that I was protected and covered by the blood of Christ because I was a child of God. After memorizing 1 Peter 5:8 in Sunday School, I dreamed that somehow Satan would still get to me since he was like a roaring lion that was prowling around trying to find people to gobble up. That made for some pretty terrifying and sleepless nights as I wondered if I had really prayed the salvation prayer properly. Had I really meant it or was I just mouthing the words? In my naivety, I prayed the prayer of salvation over and over again just to make sure. I would check my closet and underneath my bed every night to be sure the coast was clear. And I was always trying to be good because I was afraid of the alternative—sure that Satan would grab me and torture me somehow. He was definitely enemy number one in my fanciful mind.

Who is your worst enemy? Have you ever thought about it? Well, if you are a Christian, it should be Satan. He has been public enemy number one since the beginning of time. Public enemy number one, you say? Yes, because Satan wants to see nothing more than personal and spiritual defeat and death for each and every one of us. In fact, he is known as the ruler of darkness.

"For we do not wrestle against flesh and blood, but against principalities, against powers, against the rulers of the darkness of this age, against spiritual host of wickedness in the heavenly places" (Ephesians 6:12 NKJV).

Because Satan is the ruler of darkness, he glories in death and destruction. In contrast, God's ways enhance our life, they don't destroy it like Satan does. God is the giver of life—and not just our physical life, but our eternal life. God promises life everlasting to those who accept Him, but Satan has no such promises for you and me. He only wants to confuse, mislead, and destroy each and every one of our lives before his time on earth is done.

Before we go any further into our study of identity theft, I think it is of the utmost importance to insert a chapter that deals solely with who Satan is. For if we don't know the extremes of who we are working with, we will never serve God with the urgency and passion required to be victorious leaders and defenders of our faith. It is for this reason that I want to dig into the framework of Satan. We must know the ins and outs of who he is, what he does, what he's made of, what he looks like, and how he tries to deceive. We'll begin with a look at two definitions from the Merriam Webster's online dictionary for the words "Satan" and "devil."

Satan

1. the angel who in Jewish belief is commanded by God to tempt humans to sin, to accuse the sinners, and to carry out God's punishment
2. the rebellious angel who in Christian belief is the adversary of God and lord of evil

Devil

1. often capitalized: the personal supreme spirit of evil often represented in Jewish and Christian belief as the tempter of humankind, the leader of all apostate angels, and the ruler of hell—usually used with the—often used as an interjection, an intensive, or a generalized term of abuse <what the devil is this?> <the devil you say!>

2. an evil spirit : demon

If you take an in-depth look at the online dictionary, it's interesting to note that Merriam-Webster states that the etymology of the word "devil" shows that it is solely a New Testament word. Its root goes back to the Greek, not as far back to the Hebrew (or Old Testament) as the word "Satan" does.

As we look at these definitions of Satan and the Devil, several key words pop out at us. Words like: tempt, accuse, carry out punishment, rebellious, adversary, ruler of hell, and lord of evil. If you were truly aware of someone who was this cunning and dangerous, wouldn't you be warning people about him? Wouldn't you, at the very least, be telling your family or children about him? I would certainly hope so! Sadly, though, we have been deceived by our adversary the devil and live day to day nearly unconscious of his attacks—and this is exactly what he's hoping for! Take a look at what Revelation 12:9 has to say about his deceit.

> "So the great dragon was cast out, that serpent of old, called the Devil and Satan, who deceives the whole world; he was cast to the earth, and his angels were cast out with him" (NKJV).

If you are doubting the truths found in this verse and think that what I am saying is utterly ridiculous, then you've been successfully deceived by him, too! A victorious Christian life that has an identity firmly rooted in Christ is constantly on the alert for attacks from the devil. Are you aware of the spiritual battle around you? Knowing who Satan is, is the first step toward conquering his attempts to sabotage our personal identities.

Just the thought raises the hair on the back of my neck. Who does Satan think he is, anyway?! We're going to continue in our study of him and I have to warn you—at times it is extremely unsettling to realize the power he holds. Pray up and plunge forward because Satan will do everything in his power to keep you from finding this out. He is the master deceiver and the less you know about him, the better, in his mind.

What Does Satan Look Like?

Since we have already looked up his dictionary definitions, the next step that will help us in our study is to describe what he looks like. It's always good to have a face with a name, isn't it? And while the face is easier to remember than the name for most people, this is probably one connection that you won't soon forget. The Bible gives several descriptions of Satan. Though there isn't an abundance of lengthy descriptions within the texts, it is enough to give us an idea of his original beauty and his ultimate appearance at the end of time as we know it.

So what does he look like? We can get a glimpse of his appearance in Ezekiel 28—particularly verses 12-15. This passage mentions the king of Tyre, yet we believe that this is in reference to Satan because it mentions how he was in the Garden of Eden. The Wycliffe Bible Commentary explains it best. It says, "…early Church Fathers interpreted this section as having ultimate reference to the fall of Satan…" Most noted Bible scholars agree with this—as it appears to make sense according to Scripture. We'll discuss that in length in just a moment, but for now, here is this passage from Ezekiel:

"Son of man, take up a lamentation for the king of Tyre, and say to him, 'Thus says the Lord GOD: "You were the seal of perfection, full of wisdom and perfect in beauty. You were in Eden, the garden of God; every precious stone was your covering: the sardius, topaz, and diamond, beryl, onyx, and jasper, sapphire, turquoise, and emerald with gold. The workmanship of your timbrels and pipes was prepared for you on the day you were created. "You were the anointed cherub who covers; I established you; you were on the holy mountain of God; you walked back and forth in the midst of fiery stones. You were perfect in your ways from the day you were created, till iniquity was found in you" (NKJV).

Notice some of the visuals and comments about his appearance from this passage. The Lord, by way of Ezekiel, is prophesying the destruction of Satan. As He does this, it appears that He describes Satan as being surrounded with musical instruments since the time he was created. Music was apparently an integral part of his world and it is thought that this could relate "…to Satan's once being in charge of heavenly praise…" according to *The MacArthur Bible Commentary*.

The best way to know what God is talking about is to read the chapter for understanding. Let's take a look at it one more time. When you do, you will see that it begins to describe his appearance in verse 13. It says:

"You were the seal of perfection, full of wisdom and perfect in beauty. You were in Eden, the garden of God; every precious stone was your covering: the sardius, topaz, and diamond, beryl, onyx, and jasper, sapphire, turquoise, and emerald with gold. The workmanship of your timbrels and pipes" (those are musical instruments) *"was prepared for you on the day that you were created"* (NKJV).

Now imagine what he looked like. He must have been very beautiful as he was physically robed with coverings made of stunning gems. We can also glean from this passage that he is compared to the "king" of Tyre. A studded adornment such as this would be perfectly suited for a king. In fact, we would *expect* a king to look like this—any less ornate would be shameful and disgraceful to his position.

Bible scholars and commentaries agree that this reference to the king of Tyre is a direct referral to Satan himself, as previously noted. But if you think about it, their interpretation makes sense. An earthly king could not have been in the Garden of Eden because the only humans in the Garden were Adam and Eve. So it certainly appears to be a direct inference to Satan. All the other facts seem to fit together as well.

Ezekiel 28:17-18 explains further by describing how Satan's heart became proud. Because of his sin, he was thrown to the earth and was made a spectacle in front of kings and was reduced to be among the ashes of the ground. Verse 19 mentions how his life would end. It says that he would come to a terrible and horrible end and then he would be no more. Matthew Henry says that "he was hereby made a terrible example of divine judgment."

In the last days, as God proclaims His judgment on earth, we can see how Satan's countenance has changed since his splendid beginnings. Revelation 12:3-9 describes his appearance at the very end of time. Here is what Revelation says:

> *"And there appeared another wonder in heaven; and behold a great red dragon, having seven heads and ten horns, and seven crowns upon his heads. And his tail drew the third part of the stars of heaven, and did cast them to the earth... And the great dragon was cast out, that old serpent, called the Devil, and Satan, which deceiveth the whole world: he was cast out into the earth, and his angels were cast out with him"* (KJV).

Even Wikipedia, the online encyclopedia, gives the Biblical description of him as "a red dragon with seven heads and ten horns."

But the description of his appearance doesn't stop here. If we keep searching the Scriptures, we see that Luke 10:18 gives us another description of him. It says "*I saw Satan fall like lightning from heaven.*" Lightning always tends to capture our eye, doesn't it? It's quick and fleeting, yet terrifying and powerful. What an apt description of Satan. He's quick and powerful and He's able to destroy something within seconds.

These verses have painted a somewhat sketchy, yet still helpful picture of Satan's appearance. Even though the details from Scripture are a bit limited, this description gives us a glimpse of what he looks like. Although it is only a faint view of him, there is certainly a wealth of information available when it comes to his attributes, his names, and his endeavors. In the next few sections, we will look into these areas in more detail and it will probably change your idea of him forever.

What are Some of Satan's Attributes?

What are some of Satan's attributes? Every living person is defined by their behaviors. In essence, that is what makes everyone into who they are. Satan is no different. He has attributes that he has earned because of the way he behaves himself on this earth. Here is an excerpt of some of his attributes:

- He is a created being, a former Archangel, and thus is inferior to God.

- He can be only in one place at one time.

- He has limits to his knowledge and power.

- Satan cannot perform any acts unless God approves. (Job 1:6 to 2:10)

- He is a trickster and an unreliable source of information. John 8:44 speaks of him as a liar, the father of all lies.

- He is the ruler of the earth. (John 12:31, Ephesians 6:12, and 2 Corinthians 4:4)

- He leads a personal army of demons which assist him. (Matthew 12:24) Demon comes from "daimon" which means "intelligent" in the Greek.

- He can adopt a spirit form, reside inside a person, and influence their thoughts and behavior: Ephesians 2:2 describes him as a spirit who works within "the children of disobedience." John 13:2 describes how Satan "put into" Judas Iscariot's mind the decision to betray Jesus. Acts 5:3 describes how Satan filled Ananias' heart with the decision to lie to the Holy Spirit about the proceeds of a real estate sale.

- His existence places humans in extreme peril. 1 Peter 5:8 describes him as a dangerous entity, a roaring lion, who roams all over the earth "seeking whom he may devour."

(www.religioustolerance.org)

Now that we've seen some of his attributes listed out for us, let's summarize them further to get a better glimpse into what he is. In a nutshell, when we put all these points together, we see that he is a created being, inferior, unreliable, a liar, a trickster, can only be in one place, and his power and knowledge are limited.

These attributes seem to put him in his place! However, the flip side of these attributes are that he is the ruler of the earth, he leads an army of demons, he can influence and live inside a person, and the fact that he's alive puts human lives in peril. Because of this, we have to always be on the look out—we can never be too careful to protect ourselves from him.

What are the Names of Satan?

So who is Satan and what do people call him? So far we've seen how he's defined in the dictionary, what he looks like, and what some of his attributes are. But the main question that most people want answered is "Who is he?" What names do we call him? We can find numerous references to him within the Bible. Through study and through church we would probably agree that his most common names are "Satan," "the devil," "the enemy," and that his forces are commonly called "demons."

But Satan is known by many other names as well. Through research, I have found a comprehensive list of the names of Satan as he is called in the New King James Version. Keep in mind that some of the wording of his names can slightly change between versions of the Bible, yet the meanings behind them remain the same. Each one of his names has a slightly different meaning and this broad listing of his many other names will give us a fuller picture of who Satan is and what he does. Here is an A-Z compilation of his many names. (A complete listing with Scriptural references to each name can be found in Appendix 1 for further study.) I trust that you will find this quite enlightening, as I did.

The A-Z Listing of the Names of Satan

A -   Abaddon (Hebrew for "destruction"), Accuser, Adversary, Angel of light, Angel of the bottomless pit, Anointed covering cherub, Antichrist, Apollyon (Greek for "destroyer")

B -   Beast, Beelzebub, Belial

D -   Deceiver, Devil, Dragon

E -   Enemy, Evil one

F -   Father of lies

G -   God of this age

K -   King of Babylon, King of the bottomless pit, King of Tyre

L -   Lawless one, Leviathan, Liar, Little horn, Lucifer

M -   Man of sin, Murderer

P - Power of darkness, Prince of the power of the air
R - Roaring lion, Rulers of the darkness, Ruler of demons, Ruler of this world
S - Satan, Serpent of old, Son of perdition, Star
T - Tempter, Thief
W - Wicked one

If you take a moment and count, you will find that there are forty-one names of Satan listed. (It is interesting to note that there are more names given to Satan than any other created being in the Bible. Only Jesus' names are mentioned more than Satan's names.) As we reflect on this, we realize that it is bad enough that Satan is deceptive, but to be known by so many aliases, as well? No wonder we have to be on the look out for him.

What does Satan Do?

But aside from the numerous names he has been called, many people are curious about the answer to the question "What does Satan do?" Like a novel, we know that he is the antagonist or the "bad guy." We associate Satan with evil and all things that are bad. But that is where it stops for most. We fail to take it a step further in order to be fully aware of what he is capable of.

Remember back in school when we learned the parts of speech? There were two kinds of words that each sentence had to have—the noun and the verb. As we learned about verbs, we were taught that there were "being" verbs and "action" verbs. Since I have been on both sides of the fence, as teacher and student, when it comes to discussing action verbs, it is safe to say that action verbs are probably the easiest verbs to understand. Action verbs simply describe what the subject; i.e. the noun, of the sentence is doing.

So what does Satan do? There are many specific action verbs associated with Satan in the Bible. These verbs describe what he does to those of us that are in this world—especially to those who pose a threat to him—namely Christians who aren't afraid to stand up for what they believe in no matter the consequences.

Since I am a teacher, I found it interesting to do a study on these action verbs. I took the names of Satan and then compiled a list of the action verbs that were associated with him. Here is the result of that study that shows some of the actions he is capable of along with their Scripture reference. Satan:

- **Afflicted Job with painful sores**
  Job 2:7 *"So Satan went out from the presence of the LORD and afflicted Job with painful sores from the soles of his feet to the top of his head."*

- **Tempts people**
  Mark 1:13 *"and he was in the desert forty days, being tempted by Satan. He was with the wild animals, and angels attended him."*

- **Comes and takes away the Word that was sown in them**
  Mark 4:15 *"Some people are like seed along the path, where the word is sown. As soon as they hear it, Satan comes and takes away the word that was sown in them."*

- **Takes the Word from their hearts so they may not believe and be saved**
  Luke 8:12 *"Those along the path are the ones who hear, and then the devil comes and takes away the word from their hearts, so that they may not believe and be saved."*

- **Entered Judas**
  Luke 22:3 *"Then Satan entered Judas, called Iscariot, one of the Twelve."*

- **Asks to sift us like wheat**
  Luke 22:31 *"Simon, Simon, Satan has asked to sift you as wheat."*

- **Filled Ananias' heart**
Acts 5:3 *"Then Peter said, "Ananias, how is it that Satan has so filled your heart that you have lied to the Holy Spirit and have kept for yourself some of the money you received for the land?"*

- **Tries to outwit us**
2 Corinthians 2:11 *"in order that Satan might not outwit us. For we are not unaware of his schemes."*

- **Masquerades as an angel of light**
2 Corinthians 11:14 *"And no wonder, for Satan himself masquerades as an angel of light."*

- **Torments us**
2 Corinthians 12:7 *"To keep me from becoming conceited because of these surpassingly great revelations, there was given me a thorn in my flesh, a messenger of Satan, to torment me."*

- **Stops us**
1 Thessalonians 2:18 *"For we wanted to come to you—certainly I, Paul, did, again and again—but Satan stopped us."*

- **Counterfeits miracles, signs, and wonders**
2 Thessalonians 2:9 *"The coming of the lawless one will be in accordance with the work of Satan displayed in all kinds of counterfeit miracles, signs and wonders,"*

- **Lives in your city**
Revelation 2:13 *"I know where you live—where Satan has his throne. Yet you remain true to my name. You did not renounce your faith in me, even in the days of Antipas, my faithful witness, who was put to death in your city—where Satan lives."*

- **Leads the whole world astray**
  Revelation 12:9 *"The great dragon was hurled down—that ancient serpent called the devil, or Satan, who leads the whole world astray. He was hurled to the earth, and his angels with him."*

- **Sows**
  Matthew 13:39 *"and the enemy who sows them is the devil. The harvest is the end of the age, and the harvesters are angels."*

- **Led, showed**
  Luke 4:5 *"The devil led him up to a high place and showed him in an instant all the kingdoms of the world."*

- **Had him stand**
  Luke 4:9 *"The devil led him to Jerusalem and had him stand on the highest point of the temple. 'If you are the Son of God,' he said, 'throw yourself down from here.'"*

- **Leaves us until an opportune time**
  Luke 4:13 *"When the devil had finished all this tempting, he left him until an opportune time."*

- **When he lies, he speaks his native language**
  John 8:44 *"You belong to your father, the devil, and you want to carry out your father's desire. He was a murderer from the beginning, not holding to the truth, for there is no truth in him. When he lies, he speaks his native language, for he is a liar and the father of lies."*

- **Prompts people**
  John 13:2 *"The evening meal was being served, and the devil had already prompted Judas Iscariot, son of Simon, to betray Jesus."*

- **Perverts the right ways of the Lord**
  Acts 13:10 *"You are a child of the devil and an enemy of everything that is right! You are full of all kinds of deceit and trickery. Will you never stop perverting the right ways of the Lord?"*

- **Tries to get a foothold**
  Ephesians 4:27 *"and do not give the devil a foothold."*

- **Schemes**
  Ephesians 6:11 *"Put on the full armor of God so that you can take your stand against the devil's schemes."*

- **Traps**
  1 Timothy 3:7 *"He must also have a good reputation with outsiders, so that he will not fall into disgrace and into the devil's trap."*

- **Holds the power of death**
  Hebrews 2:14 *"Since the children have flesh and blood, he too shared in their humanity so that by his death he might destroy him who holds the power of death—that is, the devil—"*

- **Flees when resisted**
  James 4:7 *"Submit yourselves, then, to God. Resist the devil, and he will flee from you."*

- **Prowls around looking for people to devour**
  1 Peter 5:8 *"Be self-controlled and alert. Your enemy the devil prowls around like a roaring lion looking for someone to devour."*

- **Put some in prison to test you**
  Revelation 2:10 *"Do not be afraid of what you are about to suffer. I tell you, the devil will put some of you in prison to test you, and you will suffer persecution for ten days. Be faithful, even to the point of death, and I will give you the crown of life."*

- **Gone down to you**
  Revelation 12:12 *"Therefore rejoice, you heavens and you who dwell in them! But woe to the earth and the sea, because the devil has gone down to you! He is filled with fury, because he knows that his time is short."*

As you look through this list you realize that although Satan's power is limited, he is dead set on waging an aggressive war against Christians. And when we are trying to live a committed life of service for Christ, we have to be extra careful. He'll try to stop us at all costs.

Steps to Protect

So what happens to us when we are under the influence of Satan or are, at the very least, tempted by his schemes? Let's take a look at Jesus' response when Satan had asked Him if he could sift Peter as wheat. Luke 22:31-32 says:

> *"Simon, Simon, Satan has asked to sift you as wheat. But I have prayed for you, Simon, that your faith may not fail. And when you have turned back, strengthen your brothers."*

Did you pay close attention to the last part of this passage? Notice how Jesus prayed that Peter's faith would not fail under this attack. This is exactly what we need to do as Christians. We need to bolster our faith, so that when the attacks come our way, we are strengthened through Christ to withstand his attempts to sabotage us. We cannot let our faith fail! We need to be cognizant of God's plan for us every moment of every day. The minute, the very second that our eyes turn from God, then Satan knows he has an open door to begin his attack on us.

As we near the end of this lesson and are striving to protect ourselves from Satan's subtle influences, we need to read a great story in Scripture that perfectly illustrates how we are affected by Satan when our lives are in his grasp. Through this story, we see the importance of living a life of dedication to Christ so that none of Satan's snares and traps will sneak up on us and render us useless for the cause of Christ. Take a little trip back to the Bible times to a lake and a hillside far, far away and see how Jesus answers that question…

Luke 8:26-35 *"26 They sailed to the region of the Gerasenes, which is across the lake from Galilee. 27 When Jesus stepped ashore, he was met by a demon-possessed man from the town. For a long time this man had not worn clothes or lived in a house, but had lived in the tombs. 28 When he saw Jesus, he cried out and fell at his feet, shouting at the top of his voice, "What do you want with me, Jesus, Son of the Most High God? I beg you, don't torture me!" 29 For Jesus had commanded the evil spirit to come out of the man. Many times it had seized him, and though he was chained hand and foot and kept under guard, he had broken his chains and had been driven by the demon into solitary places. 30 Jesus asked him, "What is your name?" "Legion," he replied, because many demons had gone into him. 31 And they begged him repeatedly not to order them to go into the Abyss. 32 A large herd of pigs was feeding there on the hillside. The demons begged Jesus to let them go into them, and he gave them permission. 33 When the demons came out of the man, they went into the pigs, and the herd rushed down the steep bank into the lake and was drowned. 34 When those tending the pigs saw what had happened, they ran off and reported this in the town and countryside, 35 and the people went out to see what had happened. When they came to Jesus, they found the man from whom the demons had gone out, sitting at Jesus' feet, dressed and in his right mind; and they were afraid. 36 Those who had seen it told the people how the demon-possessed man*

had been cured. ³⁷ Then all the people of the region of the Ger-
asenes asked Jesus to leave them, because they were overcome
with fear. So he got into the boat and left."

From this story we can draw an interesting parallel on how Satan can affect our lives. Look at verse 35 in particular. It says, *"and the people went out to see what had happened. When they came to Jesus, they found the man from whom the demons had gone out, sitting at Jesus' feet, dressed and in his right mind; and they were afraid."* For you see, after the man had been freed of the demon, he was exhibiting three distinct behaviors. No one had ever seen these radical behaviors in this man before.

The first new behavior that he was exhibiting was that he was sitting at Jesus' feet. Never before would he have purposefully sought out someone that had a spiritual connection to God. The second behavior was a basic one. He was dressed! He had never cared about being modest before this encounter with Jesus. And the third behavior was that he was in his right mind. They had never seen him this way. It was such a transformation!

Consequently, we can determine that while he was possessed by these demons of Satan, he must have been exhibiting exact opposite behaviors. We can tell from our text that he was as far from Christ as he could get. He went to solitary places. He did not want to see people, let alone Jesus. Secondly, he was not clothed properly or modestly. He was chained. And he was probably filthy since he lived in the tombs instead of living in a house like the rest of society did. And thirdly, he was not in his right mind. He would constantly make himself a spectacle in front of other. But all of this changed when he let Jesus have control of him instead of Satan.

As we think about the principles we can learn from this story, we should notice an interesting parallel here. Whenever we are "under the influence" of Satan, then:

1. We won't care about the things of Christ.
2. We won't be mindful of our modesty.
3. We won't be in our right minds.

But if we choose to live our lives under the power and blood of Christ, then:

1. We will desire and seek after Him (want to be close to Him).
2. Our appearance will be modest and pleasing to Him.
3. We will be in "our right minds" (thinking and meditating on good things and making good decisions).

This is the whole point for this study on identity theft. If we don't get rid of Satan and his influences on our lives, then we will be living as this demon possessed man was. Satan is so subtle that we may not even realize what we're missing out on. How many people do you know today that see a psychologist and are on medication just to make them feel happy? They don't realize that only Jesus can make a person genuinely happy. How many people do you know who don't care about Christ and are living for themselves? How does society and the media portray our way of dress today? When you think of it in this light, it becomes clear that we are a people—a nation—that has allowed Satan into our inner circles and into our homes and lives. He's there by invitation, and he is ready to steal our identities. So how do we defeat him? The answer is found in two verses that we will be studying in more detail in Chapter 3:

James 4:7 *"Submit yourselves, then, to God. Resist the devil, and he will flee from you."*

Ephesians 6:11 *"Put on the full armor of God so that you can take your stand against the devil's schemes."*

Understanding what we "know" about Satan so far, we need to prepare ourselves to fight this battle against him. We need to be obedient to God by putting on the whole armor of God so that we will be equipped to defend ourselves against the daily temptations set before us.

Yes, Satan is powerful. Yes, he has tremendous influence. But as Christians, we have power over him. We can rise above his covert attacks because we have Christ living within us. The Bible promises in Romans 8:37 that *"we are more than conquerors through Him who loved us."* We don't have to fear Satan. As conquerors, we have the power to defeat him.

Chapter 3

Satan's Plan to Steal Your Identity

"The thief (Satan) comes only to steal and kill and destroy; I have come that they may have life, and have it to the full" (John 10:10).

Now that we have taken the time to study Satan and visualize the things that he is capable of in the previous chapter, it should be no surprise that he is usually viewed as a horrible creature. No wonder artists draw him with a pitch fork, pointed tail, and bulging horns. In fact, no picture is complete without the sinister, evil grin that sneers at those that look at his likeness. There is nothing about him that is pleasant. His outer façade, while intriguing for a second, melts into a web of entrapment. When caught unaware, we are lured by his ways and do many things that cause regrets. Take these fictional scenarios, for instance. Notice the subtle power Satan wields over us in a moment of weakness.

He glanced around the corner while holding his breath. "Come on! Do it!" he growled to himself as he watched a disillusioned woman hesitate as she held a drink in her hands. If he waited long enough, she would be tempted of her own accord. "Wait for it...wait for it..." he thought, and then it happened.

"Just one more drink," she convinced herself, "then I'll stop for good." As she looked at the amber colored bottle lifted halfway to her mouth, she battled her conscience. "I shouldn't be doing this. If my husband or friends found out about this, I'll be ruined. ...But then, they're the reason I'm doing this! Can't they see how miserable and unhappy I am?"

Satan stepped in to soothe her shattered nerves and whispered, "One more drink. No one will ever know. Just one more and then you'll feel better. You can always quit tomorrow..."

"This test is next to impossible to pass," she grumbled to herself. A sleepless night of studying wasn't helping at all. Maybe the student next to her knew the answers to this monstrosity of paper and ink that her professor had placed in front of her.

"I'll just look at a couple answers to see how I'm doing," she reasoned. As she glanced over she noticed that most of her answers were the same, but wait, those others...and she quickly erased them and penciled in the new ones. "Phew! That was close. Maybe I'll do alright now. Anyway, I deserve a good grade after studying so much."

Satan chuckled. That one was easy. She had justified her actions by herself without any help from me at all...

"I feel sorry for her." "So do I." The two women whispered. "I don't like to gossip, but did you hear what she did?"

Satan turned and left the room. No need to stick around. Everyone always thought gossip was okay because maybe they could "help out or something." Another easy target. Was his job getting easier? Or was he just getting better at it? "Must be a little of both!" he gloated.

Although the stories above are purely fictional, it's easy to put ourselves in these women's places. In fact, we have probably been in one of these circumstances at one point or other in our lives. What we don't often think about when we're in the midst of situations like these is that Satan's influence is right there lurking around the corner. He's always rooting for the worst case scenario to prevail.

Satan. He's real. His ever present force in this world can be felt and he's determined to sabotage all who will disregard the Holy Spirit's promptings. As time goes on, his job keeps getting easier and easier. Our world has begun to buckle their knees and give up the fight against him. Why? Because what he's been telling them is starting to make sense to them in their earthly, physical minds. The "narrow road" of Matthew 7:14 that we as Christians have been beckoned to follow is so hard to travel. So they've abandoned its sharp twists and turns to follow a new road—a new way of life. Many have adopted a new way of thinking along this path that they call "truth." According to this "truth," each person can believe whatever they think is right to them. And as long as we don't contradict each other, we can all believe whatever we want.

Satan's lie in the Garden of Eden thousands of years ago is continuing to this day. "You can be like God!" he arrogantly claimed as he promoted his plan to Eve. And we still believe his lie today. We can be like God, we think. Why? Because we are misled by society to think that we can control our own destinies or futures. But wait! Satan's lie gets better! Since we can control what happens in the here and now, surely we can control the afterlife. Better yet, what afterlife? I bet there's nothing after this life, people convince themselves. There is no hell. Who can prove it?

Life is just over. Or, maybe there really is something more to this "life after death." Perhaps I'll come back as someone famous or maybe even as a dog!

For Christians, this banter sounds utterly ridiculous. But to the world—they're buying it. It's what they want to hear. They are tired, even tortured, by their consciences each time that they sin. They are sick of that feeling in the pit of their stomach that twists and turns, and contorts and convicts! Much more desirable is the belief, this new feeling, that there are no consequences for people's actions because we can define what is "right and wrong" or what "truth" is according to our own experiences. The problem with this new "truth" which has become part of the popular thinking of today is it that there's no responsibility for choices made. If you can personally set the parameters of "truth," then you are also in control of the "consequences."

Along with this errant thinking comes an incredible power that's so hard to resist. For with this belief, "self" becomes the most important thing in life. And who do we love more than anyone else? Self. It's a power surge, an ego boost, an adrenaline rush like no other. We want to think we hold all the power and that we are in charge. We think constantly about ourselves and satisfying personal desires.

But the Bible's message is overwhelmingly opposite of the world's view. The greatest commandment says we are to love God and love our neighbors. It also goes on to say that we are to love our enemies. But nowhere does it command us to love "self." Why? Because God knew He didn't have to say it. We naturally take care of ourselves. "We" have become our own focus, so God, through His Word, has to shift that focus outward away from "self."

Satan knows how hard this is for us and he capitalizes on our weakness in this area involving "self." Just one little temptation from the master deceiver will get us completely sidetracked from doing God's Will. As the times around us change, his temptations don't have to be so hard hitting. It seems that just a slight nudge is all he needs to give people anymore. One push and we instantly, obediently comply with his wishes because the temptations seem to "make sense" to us.

We then begin to ask ourselves these questions as a means of justification for our guilty consciences: Doesn't God love everybody? God *loves* sinners. God is so merciful, and mercy equals tolerance, right? God wouldn't want people to suffer and be hurt, would He? Truly God *does* love everyone and His mercy is deep and far reaching. But this same God that loves so incredibly and extends such undeserved mercy has standards that must be kept—biblical laws intended to be followed.

The whole premise of this study on identity theft is found in our focus verse in John 10:10. It says, "*The thief comes only to steal, kill, and destroy; I have come that they may have life, and have it to the full.*" In this passage, Jesus is talking about how He is the Good Shepherd and that He is the gate for the sheep. Robbers and thieves will break in and attack, but only those who enter through the "gate" of Jesus Christ will be saved.

Warren W. Wiersbe explains it this way. "The True Shepherd came to save the sheep, but the false shepherds take advantage of the sheep and exploit them. Behind these false shepherds is 'the thief', probably a reference to Satan. The thief wants to steal the sheep from the fold, slaughter them, and destroy them."

You see, if we have never even entered through Christ's gate of salvation then we will not be protected at all from the "thieves" and enemies around us, particularly Satan. We won't be protected in the least little bit! Without Christ, we are standing where the enemy, Satan, resides with his followers outside the walls of Salvation. Christ's protection is only for those who have downloaded the salvation program and have accepted its terms of use. They are the only ones who have a firewall built against hell and its eternal punishment.

If we have not taken the step of salvation offered through Jesus Christ, then we are completely vulnerable to Satan and his deceptive ways. Without Christ, we have no identity for Satan to steal. He doesn't have to worry about us because we are not even children of God. But the moment we ask Jesus into our lives as our Lord and Savior and ask Him to forgive us of our sins and accept God's incredible gift for us, we will become a target for Satan. See, Christ wants each person who accepts Him into their life to love and serve Him with every area of their life. He desires that we tell others about Him, too. God is not willing that any should perish according to 2 Peter 3:9. *"The Lord is not slow in keeping his promise, as some understand slowness. He is patient with you, not wanting anyone to perish, but everyone to come to repentance."*

However, Satan has completely different desires. He doesn't want that at all! His goal is to keep as many people out of heaven as he can. He wants nothing more than to snare us and confuse us and lead us astray so that we will become ineffective and unusable for God. Satan will plant those viruses of doubt and sin in our life to destroy us and our personal identity in Christ. Satan wants to hunt us down, destroy us, and then brainwash us about the real "truth."

The minute God created man in His image, Satan's battle for our souls began. It must have infuriated him to see this manly creature that was made in the image of God. According to the Bible, wasn't it Satan himself who wanted to be just like the Almighty God, or even better? In his eyes perhaps he saw some competition between himself and man. His attempts at a coupe in heaven had devastatingly failed and had earned him this substandard means of existence on earth. But this new creature called "man" may just finally succeed, he may have thought. In fact, man even resembled God in his appearance. That was more than he could say for himself!

Now, if you know what envy is capable of, you know that it will eat away at you until you are overcome with conflicting emotions. These feelings fester and multiply until the soul that's not seeking to do God's Will succumbs to the evil fulfillment of desire to lash out and destroy.

It was probably in this condition that Eve stumbled upon the serpent in the Garden of Eden. When he saw her all alone, he finally had his chance for payback. His tortured, envious soul wanted revenge for his failure at his imagined dominance and supremacy. Yes, even Satan must believe his own lies, too. Let's take a little trip back to the beginning of time as we know it and watch the very first case of "identity theft" take place...

It was a beautiful day in the Garden. But all days were gorgeous in a place like this weren't they? Eve hadn't been in the Garden long, but it was enough time to know that she absolutely loved it here. Why, Adam was the most incredible creature she had ever seen. God had called him "man" and she was "woman" because she had been taken and created from him. Adam had been given charge over the Garden where they lived. He had taken control over all of the animals and had named each one. This was no small task, mind you, since there were hundreds of different species, each one unique and beautiful in its own accord.

And then the plant life that God had made. How breathtaking! The bushes, trees, shrubs, flowers, and grasses, their earthy tones of browns and greens resonated with beauty and perfection. The harmony between man and beast and then man and nature could only crescendo into applause for the Great Creator God.

What a wonderful God He was! He always met with them in the cool of the day. She looked forward to those times. They would walk along the borders of bushes and flowers talking about so many different things. No topic was too trivial or too broad—for God had a way of making all things fit perfectly into the exact moment and place it was supposed to be in.

The unity she felt with this loving God amazed her.

Maybe unity wasn't even the word for this feeling—for this emotion she felt springing up within her for this loving God amazed her. He was an Awesome God, so mighty and glorious. He made her feel special as if she was a necessary part of His plan and purpose for this new world.

Eve wandered contentedly about the Garden. Relaxed and in perfect harmony of spirit and soul she gazed up at the trees. Just look at them! There were so many of them and then so many different kinds. She had once tried to compare all of their leaves on one lazy afternoon but had to stop for there were too many, all so intricately shaped and sized. Adam had commented that only a mighty God like theirs could have made something so incredible for this world they lived in.

She didn't have too much to do each day, she mused, but she wasn't bored either. There was just enough time to be able to relax for a few moments here and there. One thing she always did, though, was go for walks. She enjoyed her walks with God, spending time helping Adam, and praising God over and over again. That was so easy. She knew God had created them for that specific reason and it certainly wasn't a chore for her at all. Her praise flowed fluently, continually from her lips.

In fact, the hardest thing about living in the Garden had to be the one rule that they had been given. But, seriously, that wasn't even hard to follow. She didn't really know why or understand, but that didn't matter. She just had to stay away from the tree of knowledge of good and evil because she wasn't allowed to eat from it. There were so many other delicious foods to eat, that the thought of it seldom entered her mind.

One day, when she had finished her tasks, she decided to go off on a walk. Adam was planning on joining her in a few minutes. So she began to circle the outskirts of the

Garden and spiral toward the center crossing the rivers that flowed through the Garden each time she curved around. And then—there it was. The tree. For some reason it looked different today. Perhaps it was greener. Or maybe there was more fruit hanging from its branches. That was it. There was so much fruit that its branches were overloaded and hanging at the perfect height for picking. As she pondered what God had said about not eating from the tree, the beautiful and beguiling serpent sauntered up to her.

Beautiful was not the correct word. What a spectacular creature he was. He was the most gorgeous animal in the Garden. He was almost as breathtaking as the surroundings of this great Garden they lived in. She stole a glance at him again, eyes lingering over his coverings. Every type of precious stone adorned him: ruby, topaz, emerald, chrysolite, onyx, jasper, sapphire, turquoise, and beryl all of which were surrounded by settings of gold.

"Good day, Eve." His syrupy sweetness oozed.

"Well, hello!" Eve responded, shaking her mind of her previous thoughts.

"I saw you eyeing the tree of knowledge of good and evil. What do you think of it?" He asked.

"Of what? What do you mean?" Eve was puzzled.

"You know…the RULE…the only rule here in this wonderful place." He went on.

"Well, I have never quite understood it, but if God said it, then I have no problem with it. I just get curious every now and then about the tree of knowledge of good and evil, that's all." Eve responded.

Satan jumped on her transparent emotions. She was curious, now was she? It was the perfect opportunity to wedge her curiosity into something even deeper, like doubt. For if she began to have doubts, she could be easily convinced…ha, ha! Satan grabbed the luscious fruit from the tree. Its tender and squishy softness signaled its readiness for enjoyment. He took a bite and then looked into Eve's eyes—windows to her deepest, unspoken wishes.

"It's delicious. It's better than any other fruit in the Garden," He tempted her as he took another bite. ('It wasn't better because it was so tasty,' he thought to himself, 'but because it gave a person incredible powers the moment they sank their teeth into it. They would immediately know right from wrong just as God did.')

"Eve," he began to speak audibly in his native language of lies, "you will not die if you eat from this tree. In fact you will finally live. Because the minute you taste this fruit, you will know what God knows—good and evil. Now what is the problem with that? Is He not your best friend in this Garden? Doesn't He want what is best for you? Of course He does. He won't get mad, I promise!"

And as Eve looked and lusted after the fruit he held out to her and the power it contained, she grabbed a piece and sank her teeth into its juicy goodness.

It was almost at that exact moment that Adam came near to her. In sin and in shame, she cried out to him, "Come, Adam, take a bite. It really is tasty, it's so good!"

And as Adam took a bite, the goodness that Eve had tasted soured immediately in her mouth. As she swallowed the bite, a sudden repulsion came over her. Was this what she had disobeyed God for? This immediate sense of anything and everything negative? But there was no time to waste. They needed coverings immediately!! She beckoned to Adam and they both ran quickly into the thick of the brush to weave fig leaves together…

As we gaze on this drama staged thousands of years ago, you can hear your inner voice yelling "No, Eve, don't do it. It's all a set up! You'll regret it, I promise!" ...And your voice trails off into the distance because she can't hear you. She never could. She could only listen to her own heart. How devastating that one little choice became. ...A sentence of death, not just on Adam and Eve, but on all mankind unborn, and as of yet, uncomprehending of their now dismal fate for existence. One little bite had produced utter spiritual chaos.

Oh my goodness! I can't believe it! Eve actually took the bite and then gave some to Adam. I have never understood how she didn't see Satan's trickery and lies. Why, they were so obvious! But, it's easy for me to judge Eve because I have seen the results of her sin. If only Eve had been allowed the opportunity of seeing the magnanimous catastrophe she was about to cause, I *know* she would have stopped and taken a moment to ponder the consequences. But that's the problem with Satan's schemes. You feel this incredible desire—this pressure, this longing—that cannot be quenched until you finally give in and fall into his trap.

You know, I've often wondered what would have happened if I was the Eve mentioned in the Bible. Would I have taken the forbidden bite? As I've thought that whole scenario through, I am convinced that I would have probably ended up acting the same way as Eve did, yet I'm always thankful that it wasn't me instead. Because then it would have been my name in the Bible that everyone so disdainfully disapproved of. Phew! Thank goodness!

Satan Wants to Change Our Mind about What is Right

Glancing back at our story, though, we can clearly see how Satan was out to destroy Adam and Eve. We've already pondered the possibility that he was on this vendetta because he may have been jealous of them in some way, perhaps, because of their resemblance to God. But it could be that didn't bother him at all and he was just thinking, "All right, another living being to help me fulfill my evil plans." In other words, he may have been recruiting all qualified candidates that would help him on his team.

The main point here is that Satan thought he had a job to do. He had to convince Eve to go against the one rule that God had given to them. Somehow, he had to make her think that what she was about to do was the "right" thing to do, or at the very least, inconsequential so that it wouldn't really hurt anything. You see, Satan is all about changing our minds about what is "right." In today's world, he's trying to change society's view of what is the real "truth" and he's having a smashing success with this. But individually, all he has to do is twist our morals—just a little—and coerce us into justifying our own deviant actions just as Eve did.

Satan Wants to Change How We Live by Altering the Truth

But this isn't all! Not only does he want to change our minds about what is right, he wants to change the way we live our lives. Growing up in America, we all basically live the same kind of lives when you think about it. We go to school until we finish high school or college, we get jobs, we own houses and cars, and we have families. The difference in our lives is "how" we choose to live them within these basic areas. It's the "how" that I believe Satan is so interested in. It's the "how" that he attacks through the media, the workplace, the government, and through our family and friends.

I know you've heard before that the media has probably been the single most important factor in influencing and changing our lives. Sixty years ago or so, when televisions were first introduced, TV shows focused on the family and wholesome values of right and wrong. Right always triumphed as victor by the end of the show and everything that was wrong had been made right. This is vastly different from what we view today. We are now faced with shows that depict sexual relationships between married or unmarried persons as an ordinary, expected occurrence. They also portray subtle tweaks of the moral code to be permissible if there is some justifiable cause for altering it.

This is exactly what Satan wants for us! He wants to change how we live by altering the truth of what we believe. No wonder people are so confused! Without a foundation in Christ, we are easily confused about right and wrong. There doesn't seem to be any difference between black and white because the lines are blurred. This is exactly where Satan wants us to be—in a state of confusion. Wondering what we should do. For if he has us cornered in confusion, then, like Eve, he has halfway won the battle for our souls.

It's amazing how quickly he has succeeded in this endeavor. Who would have ever thought that the media as introduced to us half a century ago would have sent us spiraling down this path of destruction? Because we know what Satan is attempting to do, we have to be on double duty as we stand against him.

Satan Wants to Annihilate Us!

As we look to Scripture for the defenses we need to fight Satan, we see several verses that give us fair warning of his attacks. The first verse that we are going to look at shows us the lengths that Satan will go to in order to annihilate us. Remember, there is nothing more that Satan desires than to destroy our every attempt to spread the Good News of Christ. He wants to rip us apart and sift us as wheat so that we will become ineffective for the cause of Christ. Luke 22:31 relays this piece of intel against Satan. Jesus is "telling on" Satan when he speaks to Simon Peter about Satan's schemes against him personally and his ministry. Jesus tells him, *"Simon, Simon, Satan has asked to sift you as wheat."* Satan approached Jesus about Peter! Peter was his personal target! I don't know about you, but being Satan's target to be sifted like wheat cannot lead to a good ending. It sounds a little messy. In fact, it sounds fairly painful to me. I don't want Satan talking to God about me like he did with Peter. I don't want Satan to ever touch me at all, let alone start "sifting" me as the verse states. But that's what he wants to do with us.

According to Matthew Henry's Commentary, "Satan desired to sift them by his temptations, and endeavored by those troubles to draw them into sin, to put them into a loss…to shake out the wheat and leave nothing but the chaff. …He has challenged you, has undertaken to prove you a company of hypocrites." This comment makes sense when we take a look at 1 Peter 5: 8. It says, "*Be self-controlled and alert. Your enemy the devil prowls around like a roaring lion looking for someone to devour.*" Satan is ready and waiting to destroy and devour us.

Ouch! Devour us! How disgusting is that! If you thought being sifted as wheat was bad, try being a little tasty treat for the devil. And he doesn't just want to chew on us a little. He wants to DEVOUR us!

My goodness, when I think of the word "devour," I get pictures in my mind of when I have been at my hungriest—especially when I feel my blood sugar getting low. I need food and I need it fast before someone gets hurt. There is nothing that is going to stop me when I feel this way and I certainly can't focus on anything else until my physical needs have been met. I imagine that this is how Satan feels in his quest to conquer us. He has this insatiable desire and hunger for us that just won't be satisfied until he has devoured every last part of our body and soul.

Satan Wants to Torment Us

As we start to wrap up this lesson on how Satan wants to steal our identity, I want you to look up a passage found in 2 Corinthians 12:7. Paul says, "*To keep me from becoming conceited because of these surpassingly great revelations, there was given me a thorn in my flesh, a messenger of Satan, to torment me.*"

Yes, he really does want to torment us! He delights in your discomfort so he persistently tempts and torments us hoping that at some point we'll give in. It is hard for us to let this soak into our minds sometimes because it sounds so "fictional" or false. But Satan is not some fictional character! He is real and he would love nothing more than for you to think that he is just a character from make believe.

Steps to Protect

As we close our chapter on Satan's plans for our lives, let's look one more time at the verse that reveals everything and leaves no one guessing what Satan intends to do to us. Once again, it's found in John 10:10 and I want you to write it out on the lines provided below. As you copy this verse, remember that this is Satan's game plan or a page from his playbook, if you will. Consequently, if we *know* what his game plan is, then he *can* be defeated.

John 10:10 _____

_____

_____

_____

Now let's list and memorize the three things according to John 10:10 that Satan has purposed to do on earth: *Satan has come to* _____, _____, *and* _____.

That's right. His whole plan is to steal, to kill, and destroy you and your identity in Christ. Since we know that already, and the Bible has told us that, then why do we allow him to control our lives in so many different areas? Just like Eve, we are tempted by one little thing and it can change our future forever. Why? Because Satan knows how flaky and fickle we are and then attacks, attacks, and attacks until we finally give in. Each time he does this, he is chipping away at our identity, trying to distort our viewpoint from God's truth to Satan's worldly "truth" that he's selling to this generation.

Since we know this is Satan's plot against us, we should turn to and cling to 1 Peter 5:8 and 9 as we forge ahead as soldiers of the *real* truth. Notice the amount of information God gives us in these two verses. *"Be self-controlled and alert. Your enemy the devil prowls around like a roaring lion looking for someone to devour. Resist him, standing firm in the faith, because you know that your brothers throughout the world are undergoing the same kind of sufferings."* Knowing that the devil and evil is an ever-present force in this world, we should turn our focus to verse 9. We find in this verse that there are three basic truths that we need to apply daily to our lives in order to protect ourselves from Satan's grasp.

The first truth that we need to grasp is to "resist him." James 4:7 supports this by saying, *"Submit yourselves, then, to God. Resist the devil, and he will flee from you."* You see, in order to get rid of the enemy, we have to resist him. And what does James say will happen if we do this? It says that he will flee from us. But we must notice that the first part of this verse says that in order to resist him, we have to be submitted to God. We can't have one without the other. We must be submitted to God so that we can resist the temptations of the devil.

Have you ever started a day without acknowledging God? It's on those days that everything seems to go wrong, doesn't it? We aren't as successful. We aren't as cheerful. We aren't as useful as we are on those days when we turn everything over to Him as soon as we get up and then continue to rely on Him throughout the day.

The second truth is to "stand firm in the faith." As we look at the sixth chapter of Ephesians, we see in verses 11 through 13 that God tells us to *"¹¹Put on the full armor of God so that you can take your stand against the devil's schemes. ¹²For our struggle is not against flesh and blood, but against the rulers, against the authorities, against the powers of this dark world and against the spiritual forces of evil in the heavenly realms. ¹³Therefore put on the whole armor of God, so that when the day of evil comes, you may be able to stand your ground, and after you have done everything, to stand."* As we look at verse 13 we see that in order for us to stand, we will have to put on the whole armor of God. We can't leave any piece off or we will become vulnerable to Satan's warfare. Verses

14 through 17 list the armor we should put on that will help us with that. Take a glance at these verses and then list out each piece of armor that we need.

"¹⁴Stand firm then, with the belt of truth buckled around your waist, with the breastplate of righteousness in place, ¹⁵and with your feet fitted with the readiness that comes from the gospel of peace. ¹⁶In addition to all this, take up the shield of faith, with which you can extinguish all the flaming arrows of the evil one. ¹⁷Take the helmet of salvation and the sword of the Spirit, which is the word of God."

v. 14 The _____ of truth buckled around your waist, with the _____ of righteousness in place.

v. 15 Your feet should be fitted with _____ that comes from the _____ of _____.

v. 16 In addition to all of this, take up the _____ of _____, with which you can extinguish all the _____ _____ of the devil or evil one.

v. 17 Take the _____ of _____ and the _____ of the _____, which is the word of God.

With all of this armor on, we will be fully protected against Satan's attempts to steal our identities. Without it, we are vulnerable. Notice how "putting on the armor" is an action that we have to take on our own. Why is it such a personal requirement that God has given us? Because, simply stated, the "putting on" of the armor implies submission to the cause of Christ. Just as a soldier must commit himself to the cause of his country, we have to commit ourselves to fighting against those who attack and defame our God.

I once heard a great story told by a pilot that helps with this second truth. The pilot explained that many times a pilot will have to fly into clouds and it becomes very easy to get lost in the "soup" because they have no real point of reference to gaze upon. When those times come, the pilot has to fight the urge to go with his gut feelings and depend solely on his instruments to guide him. He must stand firm on the truth revealed by the instrument panel instead of trusting his own gut. How true this is! The instrument panel in this illustration can be likened to our faith and we exercise that faith by wholly depending on God without wavering and without trusting our human instincts.

The third and last truth that we'll talk about is not so obvious. It is simply this—you need to know that "you are not alone in this constant, daily battle you fight against our enemy Satan." Your brothers and sisters in Christ are suffering the same kinds of temptations and struggles that you are. 2 Timothy 3:12 says *"In fact, everyone who wants to live a godly life in Christ Jesus will be persecuted."* God never promised it would be easy. Listen to 1 Corinthians 10:13 as it states, *"No temptation has seized you except what is common to man. And God is faithful; he will not let you be tempted beyond what you can bear."* He warned us from the beginning of time about the trials and difficulties that we will face, but He also wanted us to know that He has made a way of escape that is bearable. We won't remain there forever. It's an escape that leads straight into the loving arms of our heavenly Father.

You've been there, haven't you? I know I have—more times than I care to remember. Imagine with me what it is like…You take a stand for something that you are passionate about and you are sure you've made the right decision. There is no doubt. It's what God would do if He was in your shoes. It's what is morally and ethically right. But as soon as you take your stand, you suddenly find yourself all alone. Somehow all the other people around you don't agree. None of your friends or acquaintances will support the stand you've taken. At that point you're caught in an awkward moment all by yourself. It's a lonely place to be.

It doesn't "feel" rewarding even though you know you have done the right thing.

Life is full of these moments, isn't it? Despite the uncomfortable feeling it leaves in the pit of our stomach, we need to gladly carry the cross of this earthly persecution. We shouldn't treat it as if it is an anomaly, some freak of nature. Instead, we need to accept it as normal. All the while remembering that the discomfort is only temporal and no matter how lonely it feels while we are in that trial, we are not alone! God is with us! He has promised us that He would never leave us or forsake us. We can always depend on that.

So as we see the evidence around us that Satan is out to destroy us and steal our God-given identities, it becomes clearer and clearer to us that we need to stand firm and stand strong. We can accomplish all that we need to do here on this earth because we are more than conquerors through Him who loved us. He has commissioned us to stand up for the cause of Christ and to spread the Good News to our empty and unfulfilled world. So keep reading—don't stop now! Every soldier needs protection as they go out to fight the war. It's time for us to don our battle gear. Through Christ, we can fight Satan's attack against mankind and we can WIN our personal battles against him—with our identities intact!

Chapter 4

GOD'S PERFECT PLAN FOR US

"For I desire mercy, not sacrifice, and acknowledgment of God rather than burnt offerings" (Hosea 6:6).

God has a perfect plan for us. He knew us before we were even born and desires to have a personal relationship with us. He created each one of us as a unique person with distinct talents that were designed specifically for us and no one else. Only we can accomplish what He has planned for us. What happens to most of us, though, is that we get bogged down with trying to discover what God's will or plan is for us and in our quest to find out, we miss His plan altogether. En route to our discovery, we get sidetracked with less important priorities of life. Satan loves these predicaments that we end up in because they get our focus off of God. And if our focus is off of God, then we end up being ineffective. Notice some of these distractions that we commonly face in the following scenarios:

> Angela sipped her morning coffee as she pondered over her list of things to do for the day. Her list always contained incredible feats to accomplish and somehow, although she wasn't quite sure, she always got them done.

Her thoughts trailed back to last night as she surveyed the list again. Her friend had asked her what she had done for God that day and she had found that she couldn't honestly answer her. She had stuttered and stammered until she was embarrassed and then she made up some quick little ditty about spending some time in the gospel of Luke. Her list today was just like yesterday's, there wasn't one thing on it that was for the Lord. She penciled in the words "bible study" and "prayer" and then picked up the forgotten, sacred book. "Let's plan things differently today and see what happens..."

Tricia swooped up her hair into a fluffy tail and gave one last glance to the mirror. "Good enough. I don't have any more time to spend on my makeup, that's for sure," she thought. As she grabbed her purse and looked at the clock she realized that, once again, she was running late. Dodging dog bowls and ignoring piles of bills and other important "stuff," she slammed the front door solidly and dashed to the car. Out of breath, she started a hasty prayer. "Oh Lord, please understand how busy I am. I really want to take time to read your Word and pray but I just don't have any time left to give. Instead, I'm just going to take some time while I'm driving to spend with you. Just you and me, okay? That'll be good enough, right? Tomorrow I'll plan to get up earlier, then we can have some quality time God..."

Isn't Angela a lot like us? We have so much to do in one single day so we make a list and tackle it head on. Like Angela, we don't intend to leave God off our list each day, but we inadvertently do. When we're finally reminded of our mistake, we quickly readjust our list and somehow fit God back into it. But until that moment of remembrance, we are perfectly content to keep forging ahead, marking off each task, without the assistance and guidance of our heavenly Father. Tricia is a little different from Angela. Tricia has plans to spend some time with God but it usually ends up being leftover minutes sandwiched between countless chores and diverse destinations. Her plans are sideswiped by her day-to-day business.

I'm sure we have all found ourselves in one of these situations at some point in our lives. It's easy to let the glitches in life get in the way of our plans and purpose. We falsely identify emergencies and go speeding off in the opposite direction of our priorities. When we finally realize what we have done, we have wasted precious time and opportunities to accomplish what God wanted us to do that day. We could have avoided it all if we would have included God in all of our plans for the day, especially if we had put Him in His rightful place of priority number one.

It seems like I struggle with keeping my priorities right on a daily basis. Even after walking with Christ for thirty-seven years, I still find myself edging my way around God and somehow ending out in front. I have to remind myself that I am not supposed to take the lead and just expect God to tag along. I have to make a conscious plan to be the follower instead of the leader. A follower that is willing to go any direction at any time as my heavenly Father leads me through life.

I have to ask you this before we begin to move on. Do you like to have a plan when you're about to start something? Or maybe you're one of those people who don't really care and just go with the flow? Each day is different and you like the uncertainty and surprise of it. No matter what kind of person you are, I truly believe that everyone, I mean *everyone*—including all of those spontaneous free spirits out there—has to have a plan at *some* point in their lives for *something* in their lives. Certain things in our day-to-day business are just too important not to have one. A plan, that is...

Having plans is not a new concept. God's Word is full of plans for His chosen people. Knowing this gives me hope because it seems that spontaneous people always want you to think that you are in the wrong for planning too much! We will see in this chapter, though, that God's Word is full of plans and directions that should be followed and spontaneity alone is not enough. Only a careful study of what we need to do is in order as we learn about protecting our identities in Christ. This is great news to all those planners out there!

As we look closer at God's plan for us, it seems at times that some areas of His plan are very vague or grey, we might call it. The Bible doesn't seem to give as much detail in these areas as we would like. But isn't it amazing how other things in His Word seem to be crystal clear? It is on those things that are clear cut and concisely stated that there must be no compromise; thus, a plan to follow His clear leading has to be put into motion for those who are serious about following Christ. It's like God has given us a "To Do" list and we need to get busy and work on it.

I have to marvel for a moment about this. Isn't God great? He lays out specific instructions that are easy enough for even the most challenged individuals to follow. He gives us room and freedom to express ourselves spiritually in some of the lesser talked about gray areas, but on those biggies, i.e. the important stuff, He doesn't waiver. He makes our "To Do" list easy enough to read and ready to check off. I'm so glad He's like that with us because I can be pretty dumb at times. I'll need to have a situation spelled out to me and sometimes, embarrassingly, more than once. Why? Because I just didn't understand it, because it didn't make sense or perhaps I didn't get it right the first time and I had to do it again.

Of course God planned for this "To Do" list all along. He knew that human beings would need some loving guidance so He designed the written Word, the Bible, to lead us along the way. No matter what our life is like or what situation we find ourselves in, the exact truth that we need from His Word seems to jump off of the page and into our hearts so that we can apply it and begin to live the way He intended. This may sound difficult, but finding out what His plan is for us really isn't that hard. Jeremiah 33:3 says this, "*Call to me and I will answer you and tell you great and unsearchable (mighty) things you do not know.*" Whenever we get confused about what we should or shouldn't be doing, all we need to do is call out to God. He will make those areas clear to us that were once confusing so that we can live a victorious life that is pleasing to Him.

Strong's Exhaustive Concordance of the Bible gives the meaning of the word "call" from the original Hebrew. It says, "to call out to…cry…invite…" By calling out to God, we invite His presence and His help in our time of need.

Have you ever taken the time to call out to God? As you can see from the verse we just read, we need to set aside some time to find out what God wants from us. In other words, we need to plan some time to figure out our plan! What is our specific purpose here on earth? If we'll listen to God's leading, we will certainly find out.

Think back on those mornings when we made a conscious decision to put God first in all that we would do during the day. We started by acknowledging God and we sought His direction throughout the day. Because we took the time to call out to God, didn't those days seem to go a little bit smoother than all of the others? Of course, they did! Why? Because when we place ourselves in His hands to be used as He deems necessary, then we will experience incredible blessings that only come when we have completely surrendered our lives to God's plan and purpose. When we call to Him, He certainly answers us. He never leaves us alone.

It's important to mention that His plan for us is not hinged on a magical age or time in our life. So many of us have felt like it is too late to get on the right track with God. But we have to realize that if we don't serve God the minute we finish high school or college that we still have opportunities to serve Him. Of course He desires that we would be yielded to Him and would want to serve Him from such an early age, but He can use us at any point in our life! It is never too late to start.

Sometimes when we're young, God will train us for avenues of service that will come later in our lives. Ministry opportunities do not always open up right away. In the meantime, though, He is setting our stage, rehearsing for what is ahead. We can see examples of this in the Bible. David began his life as a lowly shepherd boy, and then God appointed him as king over all of Israel. The lessons he learned as a shepherd were invaluable to him as he performed his duties as king. Saul was a highly educated persecutor of Christians who found Christ later in his life. Only then did he make a 180 degree turn to preach the Gospel. His early experiences in torture prepared him to be completely sold out to Christ. He was prepared to face anything that came his way. So we see that our past can transform our future into a beautiful life of service to God if we will be open to His leading, stay plugged into a Bible-believing local New Testament church, and listen to His call.

Certainly God wants your heart and life of service the minute you accept Him as your Lord and Savior, and, yes, the younger the better. But if you are like the majority out there that have taken a few detours along the way, rest assured that God can still work and move within your life whether you're in your twenties or twenty years into retirement. He doesn't discriminate on age. And your age won't affect the ministry opportunities He has for you. If God wants you to do something, you're going to do it! He's just looking for a willing heart, that's all.

All this talk about age reminds me of a man in the Old Testament who felt that God had given him a plan for his life. His name was Ezra. From the Biblical account, we can assume that Ezra was not a young adult, like Daniel was at the beginning of his book. Ezra must have been middle aged or maybe even older based on his occupational goals. Even though he wasn't young anymore, he still had dreams to fulfill. God had plans to use him as a prophet. Why don't you take a minute and curl up in your chair and listen to this short little story set back in time around 450 B.C. in the land of Israel...

"Praise be to God" Ezra exulted as he read of the completion and dedication of the temple in Jerusalem. "Praise and Glory be to our Sovereign God!" He couldn't believe his eyes. This was really happening after so many years of exile!

He glanced back at the message he held in his hands. Haggai and Zechariah along with the elders of the Jews had just finished building the temple in Jerusalem "according to the command of the God of Israel and the decrees of Cyrus, Darius, and Artaxerxes, kings of Persia" (Ezra 6:14). As a priest of the Levites, Ezra was a teacher who was well versed. He memorized and understood the Law of Moses and his heart yearned to go back to the place where the God of Israel was to be worshipped, honored, and praised. It was his dream.

This yearning inside him to return was so strong... he had to go back to his roots in the Promised Land. He couldn't remain on this foreign soil anymore. He must go back. Knowing that the temple was ready for service now, he had to return to Jerusalem. Nothing would satisfy him more than to serve the God that he loved so much in a temple built specifically for Him.

He would begin his preparations by talking to the king. He would ask him to write a letter of passage for himself and any of the other Israelites in his kingdom that wanted to return to Jerusalem. As he humbly approached King Artaxerxes with his request, he was amazed that the king granted him everything he had asked for. With royal permission extended to embark on this journey, he knew without a doubt in his heart that God's hand would be upon them. So far, everything was falling into place.

News of a second wave of Israelites who were getting ready to return to their homeland spread quickly across the Persian Empire—perhaps spurred on because of the recent report of the completion of the temple. Or perhaps they were excited to leave because King Artaxerxes had granted such generous permission for the Israelites to return.

Many Israelites, including the priests, Levites, singers, gatekeepers and temple servants were ready to leave. They were tired of this life in Persia. As they had packed their belongings, stories of yesteryear were told in the Israelite homes. They were stories of promise, stories of blessings, and stories of protection and love that came from an Almighty God who showered good things generously upon His chosen people. There were other stories that had been passed down as well. But these hadn't been told with happy endings. They had horrified, humiliated, and frightened even the most devout Jew. But this was a new beginning. This return to the Promised Land held much anticipation. It was akin to a treasure hunter finally finding his reward. All remembrances of pain and suffering disappeared and were replaced by incredible emotions of excitement and joy when the treasure was finally obtained.

With much excitement, Ezra and the Israelites began their journey. With God's gracious hand upon their every move, it only took them four months to reach Jerusalem from their starting point in the Persian Empire. These blessings on their journey were largely due to the leadership of Ezra—for he had "devoted himself to the study and observance of the Law of the Lord, and to teaching its decrees and laws in Israel (Ezra 7:10). It was his devotion and study of the Law that had kept them safe. God blessed his testimony of honor and protected their every move.

As they reunited with friends and loved ones in Jerusalem, Ezra raised his voice in joy and praise to the Lord and said, *"Praise be to the LORD, the God of our fathers, who has put it into the king's heart to bring honor to the house of the LORD in Jerusalem in this way and who has extended his good favor to me before the king and his advisers and all the king's powerful officials. Because the hand of the LORD my God was on me, I took courage and gathered leading men from Israel to go up with me"* (Ezra 7:27-28).

Ezra was home now. His dream of serving God in His temple had finally come true. A life of service to Almighty Jehovah in his very own homeland was now a reality. Yes, he was finally home...

This is such an encouraging story of God's faithfulness to those who love Him and devote their lives to knowing Him. Ezra was a testimony to all those around him through his study and observance of the Law of the Lord. His faithfulness *to* God had resulted in a return of faithfulness *from* God. You may want to read that again. His faithfulness *to* God had resulted in a return of faithfulness *from* God.

If you ever get a chance, you should read the letter that King Artaxerxes gave to Ezra to present to anyone who wanted to stop his attempts of return along his journey. His letter gave permission, it gave resources, and it gave unconditional license to teach all the laws of the Lord to anyone who didn't know them. This letter can be found in Ezra 7:12-26. From this story in Scripture, we can clearly see the benefit of living a life according to God's perfect plan for us. That's what Ezra did, and it was evident that God's hand was protecting him and guiding him all along the way.

Knowing God's perfect plan for us is one thing, but putting it into practice is something completely different altogether. We need to factor into our plans the possibility that Satan isn't too happy about what we're setting out to do. Satan really doesn't care how much we *know* about God and His purpose for our life. What starts to bother him is when we *act* upon what we know. When we start putting our plans into action, Satan gets ready to sabotage our efforts. He certainly doesn't want us to live according to God's plan. He doesn't want any of us to experience the joy and satisfaction of living a life that is pleasing to our Lord; therefore, he is out to destroy any attempts at a life that desires to have its identity in Christ.

As I was dwelling on the question of "What is God's perfect plan for us?" I began to think about how pieces of His plan could be found by simply focusing on the word "great" in the Bible. Why? Because if we "call out to God," according to our verse in Jeremiah 33, He is going to show us great and mighty things. And if we intend to make plans for a life of service with Him, we need to do those great and mighty things during our lifetime. We can't put off for tomorrow what we can do today as the old expression says, so we're going to take a look at some of these Bible "greats" right now.

In Order To Be Great, We Should Be Like A Little Child

The first "great" that we are going to study is found in Matthew 18:1-7. Take a look at that passage with me. It says:

> *"At that time the disciples came to Jesus and asked, 'Who is the greatest in the kingdom of heaven?' He called a little child and had him stand among them. And he said: 'I tell you the truth, unless you change and become like little children, you will never enter the kingdom of heaven. Therefore, whoever humbles himself like this child is the greatest in the kingdom of heaven. And whoever welcomes a little child like this in my name welcomes me. But if anyone causes one of these little ones who believe in me to sin, it would be better for him to have a large millstone hung around his neck*

and to be drowned in the depths of the sea. Woe to the world because of the things that cause people to sin! Such things must come, but woe to the man through whom they come!"

Jesus didn't mince any words did He? He said it exactly how he felt. When His disciples asked Him who was greatest in the kingdom of heaven, I believe His answer surprised them. Surely they thought that the answer might possibly be them or some other great figure of the time, but no, His answer was children. He desired that everyone would become like little children.

Jesus mentions two adjectives in this passage that describe children. First, He called them "little" and then He called them "humble." And that is exactly what children are. They are little. Their world consists of necks that are constantly craning upward. Anyone of any importance has to be looked up to. That's exactly how Jesus wants us to be. Constantly looking up and recognizing our need of a Lord and Savior. He also mentions humility. Probably because pride and selfishness are the two main struggles of mankind. With our pride in check, we remove our own self from each situation which allows us to focus outward on others. We could sum it up this way, God wants our focus upward and outward.

We could also look at His comparison of someone who is great through the eyes of a teacher and a mother. When we ponder being like a little child, several thoughts should come to our minds. Children are helpless. They are very trusting. They are very forgiving. One minute they're upset and the next minute they are fine. They love unconditionally. They don't think about status. They are very happy. They laugh a lot! We need to be more like children with our faith—humble, trusting, joyous, and devoted. No wonder Jesus wanted us to become more like children!

In Order To Be Great, We Need To Be Humble

The next "great" is much like the first but is expressed a little bit differently. It can be found in Matthew 23:11-12 and it says, *"The greatest among you will be your servant. For whoever exalts himself will be humbled, and whoever humbles himself will be exalted."* These verses tell us that the people who are going to be great in this world are the ones that are willing to serve others and are humble in their attitude.

For those of us that were told by our parents that we could do whatever we set our minds on doing, this is quite the oxymoron. Along with that message of encouragement from my parents were admonitions to "graduate from college," "do something success-ful," and "be the best person that I could be." From a worldly standpoint, these nuggets of wisdom to spur us to succeed don't seem to fit what Jesus is saying here. Are we supposed to aim for a substandard means of existence? In my book, substandard living equates to plain old laziness. This isn't the direction Christ intended for us to go with this passage. Let's take a look at some good old fashioned principles that have been preached from these verses.

Many old timers in the faith would call the lesson to be learned from this passage the "Exalted and Abased" principle. God's Word tells us very concisely that if we want to *be* great and *do* great things we must be humble. This can be difficult at times as an adult though. If you're like me, you set very lofty goals and dreams for yourself. What we need to be careful of according to this passage is that while we are trying to reach these goals and dreams we have a very humble attitude. We should be constantly thinking of others and have a genuine concern for the well being of others that exceeds our concerns for ourselves. We need to meet the needs of others because we want to, not because we are told to. This is the type of leader that gains respect and a following from those around her.

In Order To Be Great, We Must Be Like a Servant

The third "great" that we can find in the Bible is in Luke 22:25-30. This next truth was mentioned in verse 11 of the previous passage and is spoken of in more detail here. Let's take a look at these verses together and see what it tells us what the greatest among us should do.

> [25]*"Jesus said to them, "The kings of the Gentiles lord it over them; and those who exercise authority over them call themselves Benefactors.* [26]*But you are not to be like that. Instead, the greatest among you should be like the youngest, and the one who rules like the one who serves.* [27]*For who is greater, the one who is at the table or the one who serves? Is it not the one who is at the table? But I am among you as one who serves.* [28]*You are those who have stood by me in my trials.* [29]*And I confer on you a kingdom, just as my Father conferred one on me,* [30]*so that you may eat and drink at my table in my kingdom and sit on thrones, judging the twelve tribes of Israel."*

You will notice that verse 26 is very specific about what we're to do. It starts by saying, "Don't be like that!" This is stated so clearly for us. What am I not supposed to be like? In verse 25 it tells us that we should not be like those in authority that "lord things over others." Instead, according to verse 26, we need to be like someone who is young and inexperienced and knows they have a lot to learn if they want to be great. It also says that if we are in charge over anything, then we need to be like those who have a servant's heart. We should never make the mistake of thinking that the term "servant" is a negative thing. Being a servant is the key to greatness.

In Order To Be Great, We Must Develop The Quality Of Love

Another "great," the fourth one, in God's Word is found in a very familiar passage in 1 Corinthians 13:13. It says, "*And now these three remain: faith, hope and love. But the greatest of these is love."* Notice how it says that the greatest of these is love. According to this verse, the greatest thing that we can do as Christians is love.

If we take a moment to look at this further, we see in 1 Peter 4:8 how love becomes such an important quality to have in the body of Christ. It says, *"Above all, love each other deeply, because love covers over a multitude of sins."*

Both of these references to love in these verses are from the Greek and are referring to agape love. Agape, according to the original Greek and Strong's Exhaustive Concordance of the Bible, means "love…affection…benevolence…" As Christians, the gifts that God has blessed us with should "be exercised in love for the edification of the whole body" according to Bruce Wilkinson and Kenneth Boa in their book entitled *Talk Thru The Bible.*

The concept of love is hard to grasp sometimes. Most people don't understand the true meaning of love. The only pure example of love, in all its various forms and meanings, is what Christ demonstrated for us on the cross. We live in such an imperfect and unloving world don't we? Many times, because of our selfish natures, we are quick to see flaws in everyone else around us and forget that we have quite a few flaws of our own. When we are frustrated or furious with others, we need to remember to be loving instead. This verse is a gentle reminder that we must cover everything with love and we will be much happier because of it.

In Order To Be Great, We Must Love God and Love Our Neighbors

This fifth "great" that we find ties in very nicely with the one we just mentioned. We see this concept of love flowing into a very well known discussion that Jesus had with one of the teachers of the law. In fact, some of these last "greats" that we will be looking at are probably the most obvious ones that came to your mind the minute we started searching God's Word for them.

Mark 12:28-31 says this:

"One of the teachers of the law came and heard them debating. Noticing that Jesus had given them a good answer, he asked him, 'Of all the commandments, which is the most important?' 'The most important one,' answered Jesus, 'is this: "Hear, O Israel, the Lord our God, the Lord is one. Love the Lord your God with all your heart and with all your soul and with all your mind and with all your strength." The second is this: "Love your neighbor as yourself." There is no commandment greater than these."

These verses, spoken in the words of Christ, specifically direct our thoughts about how we should love into two clear and distinct areas. The first and foremost action is to love GOD, and we are to love Him with all of our being—our heart, soul, and mind. Jesus immediately connects this with the next verse and says that we are to also love our neighbors as much as we love ourselves. Then He sums it all up with the phrase "There is no commandment greater than these." Notice how the word "these" is plural. His commandment is for both actions to take place. Love God and love your neighbor—all at once and all the time.

Looking seriously and expectantly at these passages on love, we find that if we focus solely on this one area of love and put all our energy into it, then this love will span across some of these other areas that we have been looking at in this chapter. We will find that when we love, then we are humble. When we love, we take on a servant's heart. When we love, then we can extend grace to those in need. So if you find yourself overwhelmed by God's plan for you, concentrate on loving others, and then everything else should begin to fall into place.

In Order To Be Great, We Must Tell Others About Christ

Our sixth "great" is found in a well loved and quoted passage of the local New Testament church. It is the reason or purpose we have been placed here on earth among those who don't know

Christ. If we look at Matthew 28:18-20, we will find the Great Commission. It says, "*Then Jesus came to them and said, 'All authority in heaven and on earth has been given to me. Therefore go and make disciples of all nations, baptizing them in the name of the Father and of the Son and of the Holy Spirit, and teaching them to obey everything I have commanded you. And surely I am with you always, to the very end of the age.*'"

God's plan for us is to share His perfect plan with everyone! We have been told to go out into the world and make disciples, baptize believers, and teach them the truths of God's Word. He desires that everyone would know Him and become a disciple of Christ. The first case of identity theft in existence back in the Garden of Eden could only be resolved through the saving knowledge of the blood of Jesus Christ that cleanses us from all sin. This is the first step in protecting our identities in Christ. Because man has a free will choice, we must go and tell the world why they should choose Him. He is the only protection we have against the darkness of this world.

In His last earthly words to us in Acts 1:8, Jesus echoes the Great Commission and tells us to be witnesses for Him from Jerusalem to the ends of the earth. He shows us His heart in these two separate passages by repeating the same message. The most important message He wants to impart to us as Christians is the urgency to share the message of salvation with the world. They need to know that there is a Savior who can release them from the grasp of Satan and sin. One who will protect them from utter destruction and an eternity in hell. So we must honor the memory of His earthly mission by telling others about Christ.

Jesus' words remind me of loved ones who are giving their last words on their deathbed. They know that time is short and they must weigh their words carefully so that they will carry the most impact. These words that they utter usually come from the inner depths of their soul. They are words that we need to pay close attention to because they are a summary of everything that is held dear inside the heart of that loved one. Jesus left us with His last words, also. They were near and dear to Him and of vital importance and they came straight from His heart.

In Order To Be Great, We Must Obey God's Word

The seventh and final "great" that we are going to look at is found in Psalm 19 verses 7 through 11. The Bible says here that in the keeping of the law or the Word of God there is great reward.

> "The law of the LORD is perfect, reviving the soul. The statutes of the LORD are trustworthy, making wise the simple. The precepts of the LORD are right, giving joy to the heart. The commands of the LORD are radiant, giving light to the eyes. The fear of the LORD is pure, enduring forever. The ordinances of the LORD are sure and altogether righteous. They are more precious than gold, than much pure gold; they are sweeter than honey, than honey from the comb. By them is your servant warned; in keeping them there is great reward."

This passage explains that if we keep God's commands found in His Word that we will have great reward. One of God's greatest desires for us—is for *us* to desire *Him*. I know that may sound confusing, but it rings true with our purpose for being here on earth, so let's say it one more time. **One of His greatest desires for us—is for *us* to desire *Him*.** For if we desire Him, then our lives will honor and glorify Him in all that we do.

This is, in my opinion, the umbrella over everything else we've talked about so far. We must have an incredible desire to read, seek, absorb, and follow God's Word. If that desire is in our heart, then we will bear fruit in the other areas of humbleness, servitude, loving God and others, and telling others about Him.

If we look back at our key verse for this chapter found in Hosea 6:6, you will notice how it supports this last "great" that we looked at. We see in the book of Hosea that God said He desires mercy and the acknowledgment of God rather than burnt offerings and sacrifice. His ultimate desire for us, and the reason we were created is to acknowledge God. How do we do this? Well, this acknowledgment of God is accomplished by noticing Him in every area of our lives. We know that the church answers to this by worshipping and praising Him, by studying God's Word, and through prayer. But our whole life should reflect this desire. We acknowledge God by being an example at work, by stopping to think about our next words or actions, by always going the extra mile, and by giving Him the glory instead of letting it fall on ourselves.

All of these actions bring honor and glory to our sovereign and righteous Lord and thus fulfill His "great and mighty purpose" for us. Without this final "great" to obey God's Word, none of the other "greats" would matter. For if we didn't love God and His Word so deeply and completely, then we would have no reason or passion to spread the good news of Christ.

Jeremiah 9:23, 24 supports this by saying:

> *"This is what the LORD says: 'Let not the wise man boast of his wisdom or the strong man boast of his strength or the rich man boast of his riches, 24 but let him who boasts boast about this: that he understands and knows me, that I am the LORD, who exercises kindness, justice and righteousness on earth, for in these I delight', declares the LORD."*

By understanding and knowing who God really is, we will be able to accomplish His plan for us. It takes time and it takes studying. Just like any other profession in life, training is required in order to do the job right. Fulfilling God's plan for us is no different. We need to be trained and equipped to accomplish this mission.

Steps to Protect

Knowing God has a perfect plan for us is fine, but we still

need to protect ourselves from the attacks that Satan will be planning against us. Our first step of protection should be to build a firm foundation on the Rock of Ages and start putting God's Word into practice. We need to get busy and take action!

Let's take a look at a popular story that has been made into a well-loved song for children. The story in the song tells us exactly what we should do. It's found in Luke 6:46-49.

> *"Why do you call me, 'Lord, Lord,' and do not do what I say? I will show you what he is like who comes to me and hears my words and puts them into practice. He is like a man building a house, who dug down deep and laid the foundation on rock. When a flood came, the torrent struck that house but could not shake it, because it was well built. But the one who hears my words and does not put them into practice is like a man who built a house on the ground without a foundation. The moment the torrent struck that house, it collapsed and its destruction was complete."*

We see in this Scripture passage, that before we do anything else, we must check our foundation. Is it rooted and grounded in the Lord Jesus Christ? Is it on solid ground? According to *The Wycliffe Bible Commentary*, the hills of Palestine were mostly dirt and had minimal vegetation on them. When winter's rainy season bore down on them, the violent flooding would sweep away any structures in the sand that were in their path. The only buildings that were left unharmed were those that were rooted on a rock solid foundation. As we ponder this, we have to ask ourselves some questions. What happens when it rains in our lives? When the torrents and trials strike against us, do we collapse like the buildings in Palestine? Or do we stand unshaken? We have to look inward and ask ourselves this question: "What is our foundation built on?"

Another helpful verse that reinforces the Gospels is Philippians 4:9 which says, *"Whatever you have learned or received or heard from me, or seen in me—put it into practice. And the God of peace will be with you."* Once again, knowing what to do is great. But we will never accomplish anything in our lives if we don't follow through with what we know to do. We have to get moving and do what God has told us to do!

Warren W. Wiersbe says in *The Bible Exposition Commentary* that "You cannot separate outward action and inward attitude. …It is one thing to *learn* a truth, but quite another to *receive* it inwardly and make it a part of our inner man. Facts in the head are not enough; we must also have truths in the heart. …We must learn the Word, receive it, hear it, and do it. 'But be ye doers of the Word, and not hearers only' (James 1:22)."

The second step that we must take to protect ourselves against the enemy is to equip ourselves with *everything good* in order to do His will. Hebrews 13:20, 21 says, *"May the God of peace, who through the blood of the eternal covenant brought back from the dead our Lord Jesus, that great Shepherd of the sheep, equip you with everything good for doing his will, and may he work in us what is pleasing to him, through Jesus Christ, to whom be glory for ever and ever. Amen."*

God has equipped us or made us "complete" as some other versions of the Bible read. The word "complete" in this verse, according to John MacArthur and T*he MacArthur Bible Commentary,* "is not the Greek word for *perfect* or *perfection* used throughout Hebrews to indicate salvation…, but is a word which is translated 'prepared'…" From Scripture, we can see that God has given us everything good to prepare us for the work of Christ. If we look at 2 Timothy 3:16-17, we can reinforce the point that we must be equipped. It says, *"All Scripture is God-breathed and is useful for teaching, rebuking, correcting and training in righteousness, so that the man of God may be thoroughly equipped for every good work."*

Our first step was to have a rock-solid foundation so that we will have a secure launching pad for putting God's Word into practice. But we see here in this second step that we must also have the right equipment. We have to protect and equip ourselves against the attacks that we know are going to come. Satan doesn't leave people alone when he knows they're going against his own plan to devastate and deceive the world. Satan knows *his* plan and he intends to succeed in all that he has set out to do. In order to be effective in our fight against him, we must have the same determination, if not more, than he does. We have to be equipped with the necessary tools to win against him.

The third step in protecting ourselves is to be guided by the Word of God.

Psalm 119:105 tells us that *"Your word is a lamp to my feet and a light for my path."*

Some lesser known verses follow verse 105. In verses 106 through 112, it says,

> *"I have taken an oath and confirmed it, that I will follow your righteous laws. I have suffered much; preserve my life, O LORD, according to your word. Accept, O LORD, the willing praise of my mouth, and teach me your laws. Though I constantly take my life in my hands, I will not forget your law. The wicked have set a snare for me, but I have not strayed from your precepts. Your statutes are my heritage forever; they are the joy of my heart. My heart is set on keeping your decrees to the very end.*

The psalmist had it all figured out! He had discovered the secret of a successful life that was guided by God through a dependence on His Word. Have you ever stopped to ponder the nuggets that came after the frequently quoted verse 105? Here's a personal challenge. Start researching all of your favorite verses and read the verses that come directly after them. How many of them give even more insight into the truths of God? I bet you'd be surprised!

As we summarize these three steps of protection that are necessary to fight our constant battles with Satan we must remember this: Know what we're anchored to, take action, equip ourselves, and expose the devil for what he really is—a master deceiver that's going to be a major loser in the end! Take charge of your life! With the right preparation, God will equip and guide you through whatever may come.

Remember our story about Ezra? God blessed him because he lived a life of commitment to the one and only true God. He studied and practiced the Word of God, and his life was a testimony of these actions. It is not by accident that we see his faithfulness in the folds of the inspired Scriptures. God wanted us to be able to read these words about his life to encourage us and strengthen us in our own personal times of need.

There's one last thing that I must say. As we sum up our study of God's perfect plan for us and experience this "full life" that we have been promised in John 10:10, I'd be remiss to ignore what the wise King Solomon discovered through his own personal experiences and life experiments found in Ecclesiastes. Chapter 12 and verse 13 state his knowledgeable and wise summary of the whole matter:

"Now all has been heard; here is the whole conclusion of the matter: Fear God and keep his commandments, for this is the whole duty of man."

Chapter 5

WHO AM I?

"For we are God's workmanship, created in Christ Jesus to do good works, which God prepared in advance for us to do" (Ephesians 2:10).

So many people ask the question, "Who am I?" It's a question that has always been asked and the answer will always elude those who have no hope in Jesus Christ. But for Christians, we have the answer! God knew exactly what he wanted the man and the woman to be when He created them—living beings that would honor and worship Him through their lives. God wanted to lavish His love on these new creatures and have constant companionship with them.

But Satan's agenda for mankind was quite different! Once the man and the woman were created, he finally had a target audience. These human creatures were beloved by the heavenly Father—which was a feeling that he had once enjoyed. Having lost his position in heaven and being sentenced to eternal punishment, he felt the compulsion to drag as many people as he could into the pits of hell. This jealousy towards all who are the children of God is evidenced by his relentless attacks on who we are. Take the following scenarios, for instance, and see if you can see Satan's grasp on these women's weakened emotions.

Sandra edged her way through the hall to the back of the room. She hoped no one was looking at her. The audience had been carried into the words of the guest speaker, so they didn't even notice her. Thank goodness. After she looked around her in both directions, she began to listen carefully. Maybe she would hear something new, something that would navigate her floundering existence into a port full of joy and fulfillment. But she heard nothing that seemed to help. The words that were supposed to be uplifting to her soul just left her feeling flat and hopeless.

Why had she even bothered to come here today? Her life had been ruined at a very early age. Abuse, rejection, failures—you name it, she had experienced it. Like the law of gravity, her life was being pulled downward, ready to crash at any moment into oblivion. So what was the point? You live life, you die. Only a chosen few could enjoy it along the way. The rest, like her, were doomed to be miserable until death granted some relief...

Shelly listened intently to the lesson. She agreed with the statement that we all needed to change. Most change was good or at least "for" our good—so they say. Change was really just another word for improvement and we could all use a little improving. I guess the bigger challenge for her, she decided, was not just the knowledge that she needed to change, but figuring out how she could change.

But when it was all said and done, she would never be able to change herself in the way that the teacher had said. Change usually required money. It required resources and talent. It required people around you that encouraged you and understood.

As the teacher made her last point, she turned toward the door and exited the building. "How could she change? What would she change?" she thought, "Where would I ever begin? I don't even know who I am."

These are tough emotional issues that we just read about. Satan knows that and pounces on every opportunity to destroy who we really are. Some of the feelings that these women experienced mirror our own personal life or a dear friend that we know. The sad part is that just when we think we have life all figured out and hammered down tight, the winds of doubt come along and loosen a few nails. The image we have of ourselves is something that we wrestle with on a regular basis. Who are we? You've heard it said before that even the most popular and likeable people struggle with some area of their self image. So if this is really the case, then all those people who seem to have everything in life are no different than those who are too timid to shine in the skin God gave them.

The main difference between the popular, outgoing personality and the quiet, timid personality is outlook. Each personality handles this big question of "Who am I?" in a completely different way. Because of that, some people appear to be more confident than others. But what it all boils down to is how we see ourselves.

How do *you* see yourself today? Do you have a lot of personality, or a little? Has your life been full of popularity, or obscurity? Are you a "do good-er," or a "do nothing" type of gal? Do you procrastinate, or plan? Can you joke with others, or do you always feel like the joke is on you? We're all just a little bit of this and a little bit of that. What truly matters in our view of ourselves is if we are seeing ourselves as God sees us. And if we aren't looking at ourselves the way He does, how can we change our outlook to a way that would glorify Him?

First of all, before we go any further, we need to remind ourselves that we were put here on this earth to fulfill God's plan—not our plan—for our lives. I catch myself all the time thinking about me and the things that I want to do. Meanwhile, I forget to stop and ask God if that's what He was thinking, too. And to back it up even further, I should be asking Him what exactly it is that He wants me to do—not if he agrees with what's going through my goofy head.

It's not that I think I know best, I just get busy with life and forget to view each circumstance and decision with God's viewpoint. I use the wisdom God gave me, and plunge forward ignoring the simple question, for whatever reason, "Is this what Jesus wants me to do?" I'll be the first one to say that God enables us and gives us all the tools we need to accomplish His purpose. We can find this promise in 2 Peter 1:3, *"His divine power has given us everything we need for life and godliness through our knowledge of him who called us by his own glory and goodness."* Even knowing this, we still need to acknowledge His ultimate leading in each circumstance we find ourselves in. When we can keep the mindset of constantly asking God for direction, even in the trivial things, we have come a long way in learning to depend on God.

Here is one theory that I have developed as I study through Scripture. You may have come to the same conclusion as you have studied, too. I believe that God made us exactly the way He wants us to be. Our physical appearance is His creative design, like the snowflake, no two people are alike. Our inner personality is also His creation. He gave each of us the inner and outer qualities that we need to fulfill His specific purpose for our lives. So if someone else has good looks or great talent, be happy for them! He made them the way He intended and He made you the way He intended, too. We have to accept that in order to understand who we are in Christ. If we don't, then we will always be asking ourselves the question, "Who am I?"

This reminds me of an episode of the Twilight Zone that I

saw when I was a young girl. It left such a deep impression on me. The whole story line was about a society that wanted to get rid of all the ugly people in their imagined social structure." They would capture those ugly people who fit into this category and would remove them from society and imprison them. During most of the episode, they kept these people hidden from view. When they finally showed these "ugly" people on the television screen, I was shocked! They were gorgeous by every definition of the word. However, all the other people in this society were the ones that were "challenged" in their own appearances. From my perspective, they were the ugly ones! What a lesson I learned that day about people's perceptions. The expression that "Beauty is in the eye of the beholder" never made more sense to me than it did on that day.

Believe me, most of us know how it feels to be inadequate because our idea of "normal" is based on society's criteria. Instead of focusing on our own strengths, we tend to crave what everyone else has. In turn, we become dissatisfied with ourselves. When that takes place, we find it easy to give up, or "excuse" ourselves from ever achieving greatness. How could we do or be anything special anyway? "We don't have what it takes," we lie to ourselves.

Because we are usually our own worst enemies, Satan really has a heyday. Once again, we have made ourselves the easy target. Satan only has to plant one little seed of doubt or disbelief, then we continue with the process of belittling and tearing down the person that God intended us to be. We water our doubts and nurse them for a long, long time. In fact, we practically make it our "pet project," never wanting to be away from these doubts for any length of time. This is who we are, right? Oh, so, so wrong! We are such sitting ducks. We set ourselves up for failure and feelings that God never intended for us to have. Once again, we've allowed Satan to do very little work with us. We've stepped in and taken over his job and we're quite comfortable in his position. We can destroy God's image of us all by ourselves.

This doubt and self-incrimination makes me remember a story that I have heard since I was a child and one that you are probably very familiar with as well. It's set around 1445 B.C. and probably started off something like this…

Dust clouds left a tell tale trail of where Moses had traveled. They tapered off, almost invisible, at the edge of the plain. Still a ways to go, he trudged on, stomach growling and feet weary, deep in thought about days gone by. It had been forty years since he had been in Egypt and his mind often wandered to that faraway place. The grandeur, the abundance, the ease of life, it all had been his until that day he had been so enraged by his Egyptian comrade. He had had enough. And when he had taken matters into his own hands, he had made a mess of things.

He thought what he had done was noble. He thought it was right. He thought it was just in the eyes of God and man. But in the eyes of his fellow people, the Hebrews, there was a fear of him now. Perhaps he would do the same to them? They cowered away from him for no reason at all and he had to remind himself that they didn't really know that he was one of them and why he had done it. He was their flesh and blood—not Egyptian. The dust in the path swirled around his feet as if to emphasize this fact. He was raised as an Egyptian, but he was NOT Egyptian…

Off in the distance, he noticed a strange sight. Something was burning. "The last thing this land needed was a fire to destroy all the grazing lands for the flocks," he thought. Uncontrolled, who knew what might happen with this small and seemingly harmless fire?

As he came nearer to the blaze, he could see that there was something odd about this particular fire. It was like it was self-contained already. In fact, there was only one bush that had been set ablaze. How could that be possible with all the other bushes and dry timber around?

As he took a few more steps, a loud, booming voice began to speak. A voice from nowhere called out his name. "Moses."

Who was speaking to him? And how did He know his name? But the voice continued, "Do not come any closer. Remove your sandals because the place where you are standing is holy ground."

Holy ground... Holy?...It must be God! Now it made sense. It was his God—the God of the Hebrew people. He immediately loosed his sandals and cast them aside as he continued his gaze upon the bush. "I am the God of your father, the God of Abraham, Isaac, and Jacob," He said.

Moses could take it no longer. He hid his face for he couldn't bear to look at God.

"You will go and rescue your people" God said. "I have heard your people's cries and have seen their misery. I want to rescue them from their distress and bring them to a land flowing with milk and honey. You will go and talk to Pharaoh and tell him to let your people go."

Moses was shocked. Maybe flabbergasted is a better word. Him? Rescue his people? No way! He wasn't going back to Egypt, let alone back to Pharaoh's court. He ran from Egypt so he wouldn't get killed. "Why would he pronounce this death sentence on himself?" He thought.

But instead, he replied, "Who am I? Why should I go to Pharaoh and bring them out of Egypt?"

But God listened to his doubt and reassured him that, "I will be with you."

As Moses continued to pay attention to God's instructions and watch the miracles that he would be performing in front of Pharaoh, his heart got heavier and heavier.

How could he do this? He was terrible when it came to public speaking. He couldn't do all of the miracles that God was showing him in front of a crowd of people. He would make a fool of himself—and God! He begged God to send someone else instead. ...Anyone but him.

God's anger burned against Moses as He reminded him who gave him his mouth and his eyes but then He told him that his brother, Aaron, could help. Although he felt relieved at the words, Moses felt shame. He had disappointed God. He had questioned and doubted the one true God and had made Him angry.

As we think about Moses and the guts that he had to make such a negative statement about himself to an all-knowing and all-powerful God and then take a moment to reflect on how he had told God exactly what he was feeling, I just have to wonder. It is obvious that Moses had feelings just like us. He was human. He obviously felt insecure at times, and even inadequate. *Halley's Bible Handbook* summarizes how Moses must have felt in this situation. "...Moses was no longer self-confident, as in his younger years. He was reluctant to go, and made all manner of excuses." As a young man living in the royal palace, Moses would have been incredibly self-confident. He must have been trained and educated by all of the best teachers in Egypt. But forty years in the wilderness and one murderous mistake in front of the Hebrews, had made him reluctant and fearful to go back to Egypt.

The key thing to remember here in this story, though, is that even though he felt insecure, he ended up obeying God. He stepped passed his fear into obedience. I am sure he still had the same doubts about himself as he complied with his altered job description. He still felt like he couldn't complete the task to a stellar degree. His abilities hadn't changed in this brief encounter with God, but instead of dwelling on what he couldn't do, he took Aaron's help and pushed forward with the talents he had and risked the possibility of some embarrassment and ridicule from those around him.

Have you ever mulled over what a miraculous accomplishment it would have been if Moses had trusted God the first time he was given his assignment to go back to Egypt? What if he had believed in himself the way God believed in him? Can you imagine how our story would have changed? Think of all the wonder and splendor he would have seen as God's plan fell perfectly into place. And what an ending it would have had! For God's original version, I believe, would have been perfectly orchestrated with some nail biting suspense and a climax to exceed all climaxes as Moses met with Pharoah. It's always us who try to edit God's plan and then we mess it up.

Instead of going with Take One, God's way was adjusted because Moses thought he had to have help from his brother Aaron. While still a miracle that they could approach Pharaoh on their people's behalf, it just didn't shine with the magnitude of what could have been possible. Who wouldn't have been amazed that someone who muttered and tripped over their words would have spoken eloquently by the Almighty power of God in Pharaoh's presence?

Yet at the same time that I'm saying this, I have to breathe a sigh of relief that even though it wasn't exactly as God had intended, He lovingly provided help for Moses in order to calm his fears. It was not because *God* thought he needed help, but because *Moses* thought he did. Now, if He would do that for Moses, then thankfully He *will* and *can* provide that same help for us when we need it. Praise God!

Like our last scenario at the beginning of this chapter, I am convinced that we don't live the successful, productive lives that we should because we don't really know who we are. And guess what? That's exactly how Satan wants it! From the minute you claimed your godly inheritance, Satan was reminded that he had no part of that. He is going to be penniless and defeated someday.

There will be no victory for him in the end. He is the Loser, with a capital L. But while he still has a little more time left, he's out to distract us from knowing who we are in Christ. Why? Because that knowledge of who we are in Christ gives us a power that is unstoppable, that is unconquerable, that is impenetrable. He wants nothing more than to defeat us before all that can happen.

So let's take a moment to look at who we really are. For when we see God's glory and purpose revealed in His Word and directed straight at us, we can do nothing less than stand with our mouths open and our eyes wide with wonder.

Who are we? If we search through God's precious pages that He preserved for us, we can see verse after verse that tells us who we really are. As we list out some of the most relevant verses below, please remember that God's promises to us are unending but our list has to end! So here goes...

We are His Workmanship

The Bible says in Ephesians 2:10 *"For we are God's workmanship, created in Christ Jesus to do good works, which God prepared in advance for us to do."*

I wanted to list this point first because, as our key verse for this chapter, it sums up the whole reason why we are here on earth. Who are we? We are His workmanship. He formed us. He thought about what we would look like. He carefully planned our gifts and talents. His final touch resulted in the person that we see in the mirror each morning. Think about it, we were made by Him! We were molded by His loving hands. Every curve and every corner was fashioned and designed by Him. And He made us each unique and beautiful, just the way He wanted us so that we could bring honor and glory to Him through our good works.

Understanding this first point by itself should bring closure to the question of "Who am I?" But Satan is ever ready to attack our doubts and quickly steps in to confuse us. He knows how important we are to God and he wants us to forget. He knows that he's won half the battle if we don't stay in constant contact with our Heavenly Father. We have to consciously remember that we were God-created to do these good works that He has already prepared for us. These works were designed ahead of time and are waiting for us to come along and do them. So if we don't fulfill our purpose in doing these good works, then how will they ever get done? God has specifically set aside these works for us. When we do those things that God has laid out for us, then we begin to understand our identity. We begin to feel like we have purpose. We start to realize who we really are.

We are Made in the Image of God

Colossians 3:9-11 says *"Do not lie to each other, since you have taken off your old self with its practices and have put on the new self, which is being renewed in knowledge in the image of its Creator. Here there is no Greek or Jew, circumcised or uncircumcised, barbarian, Scythian, slave or free, but Christ is all, and is in all."*

Think about this one. We are made in the image of our Creator. So when we get distracted or disgruntled by our outer appearance, then all we need to do is remember that we were made to look like God. How can we get angry at God for the way we look when we see that we are created in His image?

The *Holman Illustrated Bible Dictionary* explains "image" in this way. It says, "The Hebrew word 'image' (*selem*) refers to a representation, image, or likeness; it often refers to the way that an idol represented a god. 'Likeness' (*demut*) means 'similar in appearance', usually visual appearance, but it can also refer to audible similarity. Taken together, 'likeness' complements 'image' to mean that man is more than a mere image; he is a likeness of God."

Our image… In God's way of thinking, we are perfect. Why? Because God looks at things differently than us. We tend to focus on the outward appearance and forget that it is what is inside the heart that matters the most. 1 Peter 3:3 tells us that our "beauty should not come from outward adornment." The Bible is constantly redirecting us to look inward instead of outward.

Have you ever met someone that you were instantly attracted to? Have you ever found out later that the person wasn't someone that you really wanted to get to know after all? This reminds me of the expression "Time will tell." I heard that a lot while I was growing up and now, as an adult with children of my own, it makes sense. Give anything or anyone a little bit of time and then you will really find out what they are like. An instant attraction is usually based on what is pleasing to our eyes. There is no way to see into a person's heart through a quick glance. As you get to know that person, then time spent with them will tell you whether they are someone you want to know better, or not.

Satan would love nothing more than for us to be wrapped up in our outer appearances and to get stuck on instant attractions. I'm sure he applauds the marketing strategies that make people discontent with how they look. For if he can keep us consumed by what we wear and the color of our hair and whether we have wrinkles or not, then he has succeeded in distracting us from who we really are. He doesn't want us to be content with our image in Christ. He wants us to forget that! So time after time he waits, ready to step in at any sign of insecurity or weakness.

We are Called to be Imitators of God

Have you ever met a child who imitates his parents? It is hilarious to see a "mini me" modeling adult behaviors. But it can also be horrifying, too! Actions or words that a parent thought were hidden in the confines of their home sometimes abruptly come to light, much to their embarrassment.

Imitating is not a new art—we know that people have been imitating other people since time began. In our society, we love to imitate actors, celebrities, sports icons or other people that we think that have it all together in life. We somehow think that their life is so much better than our own. Many risk family, money, and friendship just to imitate someone that they idolize.

They don't know the freedom that they can have in life when they figure out that there is only one Person that they need to try to imitate—God.

This third point that I want to discuss is found in Ephesians 5:1. It says, "*Be imitators of God....*" It is very similar to the areas that we mentioned previously. But how do you become an imitator of God? If you continue reading verse two of the same chapter, it explains it a little further. It says that we are to live a life of love just as Christ loved us and died on the cross for us. So in order to for us to imitate God, we must show love through our life, through our actions, and through our words.

This point builds nicely onto the previous two. So far we know we have been created to do good works and we know that we were created in God's image. So if we will put "love" into the equation, we can see how doing good works will become easier because our love will prompt us to do them. When we live a life of love, then we will be focused on how God sees the people around us. We won't be focused on ourselves and how we look, we will be more concerned with others and the needs that they have in their life. When our focus shifts outward through love, then we become imitators of Christ and have embraced the fact that we have put on the image of God. We become less and less concerned about "us" and find the true reason behind the question "Who am I?"

Lest this sounds too easy, let's stop and remember that Satan doesn't want us to love. He will try to sabotage all efforts of kindness and generosity that you attempt. We have to be constantly on guard against the darkness of this world. As Christians, we have to keep that carrot in front of our nose at all times that reminds us that "*If God be for us, then who can be against us*" (Romans 8:31b). When we can remember this and live it 24/7, then we will be able to protect our identities in Christ.

We are Brought Near to God

Ephesians 2:13 says that "*But now in Christ Jesus you who once*

were far away have been brought near through the blood of Christ."
Now this point may seem a bit far fetched to you as we try to
discover who we are, but bear with me. Imagine someone who is
very famous and who you admire tremendously. As you imagine
this, think about what you would do if they were coming to your
town. For someone of that stature and fame, it would be next
to impossible to see them personally. They would have security
guards, private entrances to their places of destination, and of
course they would probably have so much to do in preparation for
their visit that they would never have time to spend with you. But
according to our verse, this Person of God, the one who should be
most revered in the universe, is desiring to be near to you. At that
moment of salvation, we were brought near to Christ—and you
can touch Him and feel His presence in the spiritual sense.

Obviously, though, Satan has a big problem with you knowing this. He does not want you to realize that you are personal acquaintances with the King of Kings! He wants you to believe the
lie that God is somewhere far, far away. He wants you to feel that
your relationship with Him is distant and hard to understand. He
even wants you to doubt that He is even there at all.

At times, we let Satan succeed in this area. Think about it.
How many times have you personally felt like you were all alone
and that God didn't hear you when you were praying? How many
times have you felt empty and that maybe there wasn't anything
to this Christianity that you embraced? If I'm being honest and
you're being honest, I think we would all have to say that we have
experienced these feelings of doubt. These doubts only arise when
we haven't been protecting our identities by staying close to God
and following His plan for our lives.

We are the Light of the World

Matthew 5:14-16 admonishes that *"You are the light of the
world. A city on a hill cannot be hidden. Neither do people light a
lamp and put it under a bowl. Instead they put it on its stand, and it*

gives light to everyone in the house. In the same way, let your light so shine before men, that they may see your good deeds and praise your Father in heaven."

Can you imagine that? We are the light of the WORLD. We have to shine so that others can see HIM through our lives. If you've ever craved the spotlight, well, here it is. God says that you cannot be hidden. That means everyone will see you. And if you're living as Christ has told us, then you won't mind people peeking. You will want them to notice what Christ is doing in and through you. Ephesians 5:8-9 talks about darkness and light. It says, *"For you were once darkness, but now you are light in the Lord. Live as children of light, for the fruit of the light consists in all goodness, righteousness and truth."*

As the light of the world, though, we have to remember that we have a very important job to do. We have to be the light for all the darkness around us. As time goes on, it seems that there is less and less godly light shining into a lost world. Because spreading the good news of salvation is getting more and more difficult, we need to shine those lights even brighter. Satan doesn't want us to shine, so he'll try to do whatever he can to extinguish our light. But through Christ, we can protect our identities by keeping our lights glowing brightly for Him.

We are His Servants, Yet We are Free

There are two great verses that go along with this point of being His servant, yet being free at the same time. The first one is in 1 Peter 2:16 and says *"Live as free men, but do not use your freedom as a cover-up for evil; live as servants of God."* The second verse is found in 1 Corinthians 4:1. *"So then, men ought to regard us as servants of Christ and as those entrusted with the secret things of God."* It is a privilege to be a servant or slave of Christ. He has done so much for us and will continue to bless us throughout eternity. His love never ends so our devotion to Him should never end either.

But ponder the cost of that love. The cost was the death of God's Son, Jesus Christ. It is His blood that has set us free. Free from the bondage of sin. Free from the penalty of sin. Free from all the things that weigh us down. Glory to God, we are free! But because we are free, we should want to serve Him. It shouldn't be a chore. We should be looking for opportunities each and every day to serve God. We can never do enough in this world to pay Him back for all that He has done for us.

Have you ever noticed how when someone does something for you, you feel indebted to them in a way? Somehow you feel like you need to repay them for what they did for you because it was such a nice gesture. Well, this is how I make the connection to this verse. I have been given freedom, but because I am free, I desire nothing more than to give all my devotion back to Him who gave me that freedom. You might ask—Is this really freedom then? But I would have to say "Absolutely!" When we reach the point of desiring to serve because of all that Christ has done for us, then it has become my choice to live in this manner, not my mandate.

Now, before we forget this point, we have to realize that Satan is definitely going to come along and try to distract us as we serve the Lord. He wants us to assume the mind set that we are "owed" the blessings that we receive from God and, therefore, we don't really need to serve Him all of the time. Beware of his tactics! Even a life of 100% service to God could never repay the eternity in heaven we will be given as Christians. This is just one other way that Satan wants us to forget our identity.

We are a New Creation

We all like new things, don't we? There's just something about having a sealed wrapper or a tag on what you get. It means that what you're about to savor and enjoy has been unused by anyone else. It is fresh, it is clean, it is without blemish and you will be the first one to relish in its newness. If something happens to that new object, then you will be the only one to blame because you are responsible for its upkeep. 2 Corinthians 5:17 talks about new things. It says "*Therefore, if anyone is in Christ, he is a new creation; the old has gone, the new has come!*" According to this verse, we all have a second chance at making things new again. The moment that we accept Christ as our Savior we become a new person. We get a fresh start.

Ephesians 4:22-24 explains this a little more. It states that "*You were taught, with regard to your former way of life, to put off your old self, which is being corrupted by its deceitful desires; to be made new in the attitude of your minds; and to put on the new self, created to be like God in true righteousness and holiness.*"

New things have more value, don't they? They usually cost more than something that is old or used because of their new condition. We are a lot like this as believers. Once we accepted Christ's atoning blood, we became new, clean, and priceless to Him. Only problem is, Satan doesn't like us to feel brand new. He wants us to feel cheap, used up, and worthless. He wants us to keep remembering the past and live a defeated life. But Satan can't get us down unless we let him because of what Ephesians has to say—the old has gone, the new has come! We can be excited about this truth because we are now worth more than we ever were before. Our lives truly matter because we are a new creation.

We are His Children Which Makes Us His Heirs

We are heirs to the king! How do we know? Because Galatians 3:26 tells us this: "*You are all sons of God through faith in Christ Jesus.*" Verse 29 follows saying, "*If you belong to Christ, then you are Abraham's seed, and heirs according to the promise.*" But this isn't the only verse that mentions this. Read two more verses that show us that we are indeed heirs of God. Romans 8:17 says "*Now if we are His children then we are heirs—heirs of God and coheirs with Christ, if indeed we share in his sufferings in order that we may also share in his glory.*" Titus 3:7 also supports our point by saying, "*So that, having been justified by His grace, we might become heirs having the hope of eternal life."* It is our faith in Jesus Christ that makes us heirs to the King.

Just imagine being a child and an heir of the Almighty God. There is no one more powerful than He. There isn't anyone who can defeat or destroy Him. Because of our position in Christ—God's family, we are incredibly blessed. If you secretly crave status, then here it is. You can't move any higher up the ladder than this.

As we take this point to heart and ponder the reality of our status in Christ, we again have to be on guard against Satan's attacks. He doesn't want us to figure out that we have the army of the Lord on our side. He doesn't want us to know that as direct heirs to the throne, we have been surrounded by angels to guard our every step. He prefers that you feel alone and insignificant. He doesn't want us to claim our heavenly inheritance. Once again, we have to protect our identities, because this is one identity I don't want to give up easily!

We Were Chosen to be Saints

Colossians 1:24-29 says *"Now I rejoice in what was suffered for you, and I fill up in my flesh what is still lacking in regard to Christ's afflictions, for the sake of his body, which is the church. I have become its servant by the commission God gave me to present to you the word of God in its fullness—the mystery that has been kept hidden for ages and generations, but is now disclosed to the saints. To them God has chosen to make known among the Gentiles the glorious riches of this mystery which is Christ in you, the hope of glory."*

Because of what Christ did on the cross for us, we can be called saints. Satan doesn't want us to grasp this point because he'd rather have us feeling worthless. He doesn't want us to ever feel "good enough" to have deserved God's unmerited favor. But no matter what Satan would like, we are saints anyway!

Now I know what you're thinking. I am not a saint! Or maybe you're thinking, YOU are not a saint! Regardless of what you may think, we have been covered in robes of righteousness at salvation and God sees us as saints. Imagine that! Saint Karen, Saint Laura, Saint Lindsey, Saint _____. This is by no means a mockery of the term, just an incredible awareness of my likeness in Christ. Because we accepted what He did for us two thousand years ago, our mirror reflects this saintly image that may seem foreign to us at times, yet it holds an unmistakable resemblance to ourselves. How thankful I am for those robes of righteousness.

What is also so amazing is the fact that we are chosen by God to be His saints. Doesn't the very thought of that make you sit up a little straighter? We weren't some random accident or a just another quick pick. No, we were chosen. It was thought out thoroughly and carefully and then we were lovingly selected by God.

As a woman, this reminds me of shopping. Now think about this with me… When you are going to purchase something of value, you are very careful. You weigh every decision. You look at the pros and cons. You look at the price and consider what you are getting in exchange. You then decide if it is worth the price you will pay. Aren't we blessed to have been selected by God because even though He saw that we had flaws, when the "pros" were stacked against the "cons," our "pros" came out slightly ahead. I am so thankful that God thought we were worth it!

We are Royalty

God's Word says in 1 Peter 2:9, "*But you are a chosen people, a royal priesthood, a holy nation, a people belonging to God, that you may declare the praises of him who called you out of darkness into his wonderful light.*'

Jesus is the King of Kings and the Lord of Lords! As His child that makes me royalty. I am a princess and will someday become his queen at the marriage supper of the Lamb. A queen? Can you imagine? It's kind of hard, I know. Having come from lowly roots, it's almost unfathomable to daydream of that day when I will don my white robes and feast with my heavenly Groom, the King of Kings. There is no way that I could have attained such a position on earth. Yet in heaven, I will be exalted to that glorious position. All because one day I made a decision to let Christ change my life by becoming my Lord and Savior. All of this can be yours, too. God is not a respecter of persons. This royalty that He has given to me, He will gladly give to you. All you have to do is ask Him into your heart and life.

Steps to Protect

As we think about all of these things that we are in Christ and because of Christ, we would be foolish to think about these blessings lightly. These gifts of "who we are" need to be treasured. We should remind ourselves every day of the blessings we have because of who we are in Christ. As we have said, over and over again, we can't let Satan try to convince us that we are anything else. So, in closing, it would be a mistake to not take this knowledge just one step further. We can never take too many precautions to protect our identities in Christ.

Remember the key verse for this chapter? It is *"For we are God's workmanship, created in Christ Jesus to do good works, which God prepared in advance for us to do"* (Ephesians 2:10). We have been created to accomplish the will of God. We have been equipped to bring glory to His name. We have been supplied with all the essential tools that we need in order to serve Him while we are on this earth. Whenever you start to doubt your abilities, take a look at this list of reminders of who you are in Christ. Post them somewhere around your house and reflect on them when you begin to doubt who you are:

Remember…

1. If I am His workmanship, then I can do whatever He wants me to do.

2. If I am made in His image, then I shouldn't complain about my looks.

3. If I am an imitator of God, then I can serve Him as Jesus did.

4. If I was brought near to God, then I can go to Him whenever I need to.

5. If I am the light of the world, then I can shine for Jesus.

6. If I am His servant, then I will do great things for Him.

7. If I am free, then I can live for Him without holding anything back.

8. If I am a new creation, then I have value and great worth.

9. If I am His child, then He is my Father.

10. If I am His heir, then I will never lack anything.

11. If I am chosen, then I am special to God.

12. If I am a saint, then I can live with Him in eternity.

13. If I am royalty, then I have been given everything!

Only a gracious and loving Lord would have taken the time to pass on so many beautiful analogies to His loved ones. Take a moment and soak it all in. We are incredibly special to God. We mean absolutely nothing to Satan. Through our loving heavenly Father, we can keep our identities protected through every road in life. His love and provision for us is a priceless gift to be treasured until He comes again.

Chapter 6

MY WALK WITH GOD

"He has showed you, O man, what is good, and what does the Lord require of you? To act justly and to love mercy and to walk humbly with your God" (Micah 6:8).

Once we've accepted Christ as our personal Savior, we often find ourselves asking the question, "What's next? What am I supposed to do along this Christian journey?" If you are like me, you probably want a list or set of rules to follow so that you can be sure to do the right thing as a new believer.

Well, the Bible is full of answers to our questions, but I think the specific answer to this particular question can be summed up best by looking at our featured verse for this chapter found in Micah 6:8. This verse tells us exactly what God requires of us. It tells us that we are to act justly. We are to be honest and just in all that we do so that others will see a difference in our lives as compared to those around us. It also tells us to love mercy. Our world can be a mean spirited place to live. If we show mercy, then those that are unsaved will notice a different pattern of behavior in us. Instead of insults or anger, we should extend mercy. Lastly, the verse tells us to walk humbly with God. Notice that it didn't tell us to walk with God—it said to walk humbly with our God. Why include the adverb? Because God wants us to know how to walk—humbly.

Our Christian journey isn't always going to be easy or make sense. The one thing that we have to do, though, whether we are new Christians or old, is to get into the Word each and every day. We will never understand our complete purpose in life if we don't find out what God has written down for us.

Reading God's Word is important! For many years I didn't think it mattered how little or how much I read of His Word. At times I had a casual relationship with God. I put my Bible study on a "need to know" basis. But through the years and through the mountains and valleys of life, I have always found that my journey goes better when I am completely familiar with my road map—the Bible. So as we think about our walk with God in this chapter, I encourage you to look at these next three scenarios and decide what kind of Christian are you.

Jen glanced around the room to see if she had forgotten anything. She skimmed her eyes across her shelf and momentarily paused at the leather bound book. She knew it should be off the shelf and by her bed so that she could remember to read it, but there it sat. Someday I'll move it. Maybe even some day I'll read it. God knows how busy I am with work and all, besides, you would think a loving God like Him would understand if she didn't really feel like reading it anyway. Someday she'd get around to it. Just not now…

"That was interesting," Bethany mused as she closed her devotional book and laid it on the nightstand, "I never thought about it quite that way." As her head fell back on the pillow, she closed her eyes and continued her ponderings. God was good and He desired that she loved Him with her whole heart, the readings had said. She did love God and was truly grateful for His Son's sacrifice, in fact, all throughout the day she continuously acknowledged

His presence in her life. But what did He really mean by saying her "whole" heart? She already loved God with everything, right? Just by the fact that she constantly thought of Him proved that, or did it? Actually, I guess it didn't. God wanted more, so much more, and she wasn't sure she was willing or had the time to go that far with Him. At least she spent a little bit of time with Him each day...

Marty shut her study guide so hard that it knocked her pencil onto to floor. "That was awesome!" she thought, "How come she had never seen that before? She had read that passage so many times but it had never said that—or, did it? God's Word was the most incredible piece of literature she had ever studied. It was the only Book she knew that offered advice, recited her deepest thoughts, gave her specific directions, comforted her raging emotions, and tugged at her heart to read even more. It was brilliant, really. Only a marketing savvy Author could pack all that into one book, and instead of writing sequels, kept prompting the heart to read the same stories over and over again.

Maybe you could identify with one of those scenarios because at some point in your walk with God you have probably been like one of these people. Sometimes we are more on fire for God than other times. Wouldn't you agree? We may start out flickering in our faith, but when we stay in constant communion with God, we grow into a bonfire that glows in a continual, steady flame of warmth and oneness with God. Other times it seems that we fan the same flame and it shines brightly for a little while but then it simmers down and has to be fanned again to get it going. Sometimes, though, we don't even feel like lighting a fire at all, we're enjoying the cool air around us and want to linger in this spot for just a little while longer. We can just grab a sweater to warm our cold hearts and then we can light the fire later. This last place is exactly where Satan wants you to be. He wants your focus to be in the opposite direction so you won't see the goodness of God in front of you.

In the area of personal priorities, Satan's identity theft conspiracy is doing double duty. He doesn't want you to experience that personal surrender to God that sends you climbing toward the summit of fulfillment and happiness that affects every area of your life. When you think about a Christian that you know who always seems to have it together, you notice that their priorities are always in order. They don't seem to get distracted by the things around them. So, if we want to be like them, it would seem logical that we need to get our own priorities in ship shape. That can be quite a struggle. It's actually not that easy to do.

Why does everything worthwhile have to be so hard to attain? Have you ever thought about why it's so difficult to keep everything functioning the way it should? And the harder you try, the more it seems that you fail. This old flesh that wraps around us tightens its hold on us at just the most inopportune times. We truly want to do what's right in our hearts but we get this cramp in our style that has to be massaged and worked out and by the time that gets fixed we forget what we were originally planning to do—focus some time on God.

God's Word deals with these mental and physical struggles of ours. He has given us many verses that address this exact issue. Let's go back to Micah 6:8 again because he packaged it so perfectly.

> "He has showed you, O man, what is good, and what does the Lord require of you? To act justly and to love mercy and to walk humbly with your God."

Let's break it down differently this time. In the first part of the verse, it tells us two distinct things that we have to recognize. The first one we have to recognize is that God has shown us what is good. You don't have to wonder what is good because He's already shown us. It's right there in black and white. The school teacher has to come out in me right here. I can't even tell you how many times I have explained a new concept to my students only to have them raise their hand the minute I finish and innocently ask me to explain the exact same thing again because they weren't listening. My mind is scolding "Weren't you paying attention??? I just taught all of this!" while my mouth dutifully recites it once again. I have to think that this must be a little bit of how God must feel. He has told us about all these good things that we have been given, He's explained how to use them, and we aren't even paying attention. When we finally decide to listen, He's just finishing up His lesson and we missed it all. All these good things that we are seeking can be found in the Scriptures, but until you pay attention to them, you will never know what they are.

The second thing that we must recognize from this verse is that He tells us what He requires from us. He doesn't play guessing games. He is always going to shoot straight. Now "requires" is a very strong word, isn't it? It doesn't mean what God prefers, what He would like, or what you could choose. According to Strong's Exhaustive Concordance of the Bible, it refers to "seek or ask," specifically in the area of worship. No, God is not sitting around telling us "it would be nice if you would do this or that..." No, (and thank goodness) He just tells us like it is. This is what I am asking of you. This is what I require and this is how I want you to do it. So if we genuinely want to know what God wants, all we have to do is finish studying the verse.

The last section of the verse lists three simple things that God requires. The first requirement is "To act justly." This isn't that hard to do. Simply put, just do what is morally and ethically right. Follow the basics of the Ten Commandments. And in doing so, love God and love your neighbors. It is our tendency to sin and our weakness to resist the sin that complicates this first point.

The second requirement that our verse gives is "to love mercy." What is mercy? The Merriam-Webster's Online Dictionary defines it as "a compassion or forbearance shown especially to an offender or to one subject to one's power." If we have mercy, then we won't be so judgmental and condemning of others. We will be like the Good Samaritan. We will be merciful like Jesus was while He was here on earth.

The third and last requirement says "to walk humbly with your God." We should live everyday as if God was walking right beside us. Knowing that He is all seeing and ever present will change our every action.

Our walk with God can literally be that easy. God knew we couldn't remember a great big old long list so He summed our walk with Him up into those three basic areas just like an outline from a good, Bible-believing preacher. Three points. Not too many and not too few. Just enough for our simple minds to process, understand, and remember. When we can finally live most of each day following these steps, we will find a closeness with God that many around us will never experience because they don't want to take their focus away from themselves.

Micah isn't the only place in the Bible where we can find these nifty lists of things to do. We find more in Deuteronomy, Ecclesiastes, Proverbs, the Gospels, and the Epistles of Paul. The lists are there throughout the Old and the New Testaments. If you only like reading the New Testament, then you'll eventually stumble over them. If you're digging through the Old Testament, then you will see them laced through many of the stories of the major Bible characters. You can copy them and tape them to your bathroom mirror as a daily reminder of what God desires from you.

All of this is great, but like anybody, we won't do something that seems difficult unless there's some sort of benefit from it. Take exercising, for instance. The only reason we set aside time to exercise is because we know that we need to do it in order to keep our body healthy and functioning the way it should. Or what about a project that's due at work or at school? We sit there in agony over the topic until we finally have collected enough words and have placed them in just the right order to fill up the exact number of pages we need. Nothing more, nothing less. Just enough to get by—unless you're into that kind of thing.

Our walk with God can be just like that. Until we see the immediate and eternal benefits, we don't have any inner desires to make a change in what we're doing. This reminds me of a story of a man who went the extra mile and daily died to his personal desires. He put self aside and lived a life that was a steady journey with God. There were hills and valleys along the road, but his triumphs were testimony to a life that was wholly committed to God. God revealed many classified secrets to him because He knew he could be trusted. His devotion proved it. If only we could live a life that God saw worthy of giving top secret clearance to—a life where the mysteries of the Scriptures were fully revealed because of a hunger, desire, and dependence on Christ.

This Bible character that I'm writing of is Daniel. If you've been in church for a good part of your life, you might even remember a song that was sung about him. It was called "Dare to Be a Daniel." It went on to say in one line of the song that we needed to "Dare to stand alone..." You probably know how he stood up to the king's diet that went against Jewish kosher laws, how his friends went into the fiery furnace, and how he landed himself in the lion's den because he wouldn't stop praying to the one true God. However, this next story about him, found in Daniel 10, may be a little unfamiliar, yet it reveals why God chose him to be part of Scripture's story...

Daniel opened his journal and began to write,

"It is the third year of King Cyrus of Persia's reign and I have been in mourning for three weeks now because of a revelation that God has given to me. I haven't eaten at all since this vision came to me. No meat or wine has touched my lips. I haven't used any lotions at all since I received the disturbing news. My skin is so dry and tortured because of my thirst. I am not worthy to know so much of God's plans for the future. I don't understand why He is entrusting this knowledge to me, yet He does. So I take up my pen and write it down. Then I mourn and weep for what is to come. I pray for forgiveness for myself and for Israel. Please hear our cries, O Lord. We make these requests not because we deserve them, but because you are a merciful God…"

As I put away my writing instruments, I wondered if I would ever understand the meaning of this last revelation. Understanding often brought fear, for God's future plans that He was revealing to me were usually full of terror and destruction. Even when they were explained, the weight of God's impending doom crushed my spirit, prompting me to pray and fast even more than I already did for my wayward people.

Today was the twenty-fourth day of the first month. My stomach had stopped growling two weeks ago and I rarely even thought about eating anymore, except when my neighbor would cook some loaves for their supper, then the aroma tempted me of tasty treats. Otherwise, all that consumed my body and soul was the meaning of this new revelation which sent me to my knees to cry out for mercy and pardon from the Almighty God.

In an effort to clear my churning mind, I decided to take a walk. There were many beautiful places to stroll around my neighborhood. The Tigris River wasn't far and I always enjoyed taking jaunts along its rushing banks. As I stepped carefully off the path and into the river's flora

I remembered why I had eventually grown to appreciate this new land. It had a beauty different from my motherland, yet it still reminded me of home. Someday I hoped to go back—as soon as the seventy years of exile were ended.

Suddenly, as I was walking, the strangest scene emerged along the bank. Directly in front of me was a man dressed in linen with a belt made of the finest gold. There was nothing odd about the man until my eyes lifted to his face. It was almost indescribable! His face lit up like lightning and his eyes were like burning flames of fire. His arms and legs were toasted in bronze perfection. It was hard to keep a steady gaze on him because of the intensity of light reflecting from within him. As he began to speak to me, I almost covered my ears from the booming voice that sounded as if a great crowd was speaking in unison.

I looked around me from the left to the right. Was anyone else seeing this or hearing this? Or was I imagining this fearsome sight? The men with me saw nothing, yet they turned and ran in terror, hiding from a horror they could only feel in their bones. And there I stood, alone and defenseless, in front of this man. My face drained of its color and my body refused to move. What I willed it to do, it wouldn't. Each of my limbs hung disobediently by my side. I was helpless. What else could I do but listen as my body melted prostrate to the ground in a deep sleep?

In the next moment, I unwittingly recoiled as a hand guided me to my knees. I was trembling now, not sure of what would happen next. Yet for some unknown reason, as the man began speaking, I felt a calm come over me and I felt compelled to strain forward to capture every word. Somehow this frightening man put me immediately at ease. He told me that he had come to me because

I was highly esteemed and needed to carefully consider the things he was about to tell me.

I was standing again by this time, but my legs were still unsteady beneath me. I felt as if I could sink yet walk on water all at the same time. In a dream, anything could happen...

He told me not to be afraid, and then he spoke my name. He knew me. He knew everything about me, so I listened even more closely to his message. I had been chosen to receive this revelation and vision because I had been faithful. From the very first day in my walk with God I had desired only to gain a deeper understanding of His ways. He also said I was chosen because I was humble. Me? I hadn't really ever thought about that, but I guess I must be or he wouldn't have said it. He then told me that he had come in response to my prayers. My prayers and my journal? He knew of my agonizing thoughts? He had heard my cries and came to find me in the midst of my distress.

I was speechless as he explained this new revelation that had been given to me. The weight of it all bore down on me like a giant boulder—smothering and smashing. Who was I? Why was he telling me these things? I was helpless and useless. How could I bear this anchor tied to my soul?

As if hearing my thoughts, he reached out toward me and strength flowed through his touch. Again, he told me not to be afraid, then he admonished me twice to be strong as he finished foretelling the events to come.

As I sat journaling that night, my crashing thoughts rammed against the walls of my mind. The heaviness of it all suffocated me yet prompted my pen to continue. I must write what God had shown me today—whether or not it made sense to me did not matter. I was the vessel He had chosen to disclose this wonder. As I paused in prayer, mid-sentence, I thanked God for His mercy toward me. Uncomprehendingly, yet all-knowingly, I began to understand. God was revealing these things to me because I had been proven faithful. I had desired Him to be part of my entire being each day, I prayed to Him, and in return, He was using me to carry on His purpose.

I sometimes try to imagine what it might have been like if I were Daniel. He seemed so brave and confident even when he was away from all that was familiar to him. When I am away from familiar landmarks or find myself in a new and uncomfortable situation, I begin to get butterflies in my stomach and a sense of insecurity begins to envelope me. But Daniel did not seem to suffer from any of my insecurities. Instead, He was firm with conviction while he stood in front of a king. He was steadfast and calm as he gazed into the whites of the hungry lion's eyes. He was respected by God in such a way that he was chosen to be one of the inspired writers of the Old Testament. He was trusted with visions of unforeseen wars that would take place centuries and millenniums later.

If I were Daniel or you were Daniel, then we could have done the great things that he did. But could we, in our faith as it is right now in the twenty-first century, have stood up to the challenge? Is our faith today as strong as Daniel's of yesteryear? Such questions should prompt us to dig deeper, read more, and never quit this journey with Christ that we take on a daily basis. Perhaps someday we will be deemed as worthy as some of these honored men and women of the Bible.

I don't want to sound presumptuous or prideful here, but when you break down the elements of Daniel's worthiness, it actually seems as if it could be attainable for us. In fact, 2 Peter 1:3 tells us:

"His divine power has given us everything we need for life and godliness through our knowledge of him who called us by his own glory and goodness."

When we look up the meaning of the word "everything" or rather, "all" things as it is referred to in the King James Version, we find that it is a reference to "…any, every, or the whole…" according to Strong's Greek dictionary. In other words, there is nothing that we lack to make us a better Christian or to do great things for God. It is completely possible in the twenty-first century to do incredible things for God's honor and glory!

In Daniel 10, where this story is found, it lists the reasons he was chosen as an inspired vessel of God. Verse 8 of this chapter said that he was helpless. *"So I was left alone, gazing at this great vision; I had no strength left, my face turned deathly pale and I was helpless."* From what we know, Daniel had many times in his life when he felt that he was helpless. The very fact that he had been captured and taken to Babylon proved that he had been helpless. Being helpless isn't always a bad thing. In fact, I am trying to show here that in God's eyes, it's a must. We must first be helpless, totally incapable of existing on our own, before God can begin to use us. Only when we surrender every last survival tool that belongs to us will God step in and do a miracle in our life. It's hard to give it up, though, because we think we can't live without something tangible to hold on to. But according to God's methodology, we have to give it all up first. We have to leave everything behind so that we can follow Christ. So as we look back at out story, we see that Daniel was lying flat on the ground beside the mighty Tigris River completely helpless—yet at the same time, completely usable before God.

Verse 12 gives us even more insight to Daniel's credibility with God. It says, *"Then he continued, 'Do not be afraid, Daniel. Since the first day that you set your mind to gain understanding and to humble yourself before your God, your words were heard, and I have come in response to them."*

According to this verse, Daniel set his mind to knowing God. He didn't want a cordial, surface relationship with this God of his. He wanted to know His ins and outs, the whys and the hows. I believe it was this deep seeded desire to somehow understand an unexplainable God that brought about his humbleness of heart. How could you approach the inner chambers of the Almighty and not fall flat on your face like Daniel did beside the Tigris River? For Moses, as he stood in front of the burning bush, it was impossible to remain standing; and for Daniel, it could be no different.

Before we move on from this verse, there is an important truth to discover in the last two phrases of "...*your words were heard, and I have come in response to them..*" John MacArthur explains it this way. "This was a great encouragement from God who was attentive to prayer and acted to answer it." God paid special attention to Daniel's prayers because he had chosen to set his mind on Him—no matter the cost or the inconvenience.

In verses 16 and 17 of chapter 10, Daniel mentions again that he is helpless, then he adds that he is just a servant. Like Daniel, this is how we too can become usable for God. We need to get rid of all our selfish, hidden desires and replace them with the energizing batteries of God's power. Only then, like Daniel, will we operate as God intended. Our once lifeless, yet busy, existence can now be synchronized to serve by the movement of God.

Let's recap the steps that Daniel took:

- He knew he was helpless before an Almighty God.

- His wonder for this awesome God made him want to get to know Him better.

- As he learned more about this God of his, he could do nothing but humbly love and serve Him.

- This humbleness translated to a feeling of helplessness because he knew he was nothing without God.

As we look at this progression in Daniel's life, I have to think "If only we could be more like Daniel!" But as I look into God's

Word, I realize that we can! Satan hates this way of thinking. He attacks it. He defies it. He wants to try and convince us that we really aren't capable of doing the same things we read in the Bible. Satan wants us to say "I can't" instead of "I can."

But no matter what Satan tries to do, I am convinced that with God's power we can accomplish as much, if not more, than what we read within those sacred pages. These mighty men of God were human just like us. They sinned just like us. They had to deny themselves daily just like us. With God's help, we can accomplish feats just as great as they did! The only difference is that our accomplishments won't be written down inside the inspired Word of God for others to read. When we finally realize that our walk with God can be as incredible as a Bible hero's, then God's supernatural empowerment can change our lives. Satan—this is one identity we don't ever want to surrender to you! You can try to steal it, but our firewall in Christ is indestructible. We are complete in Him.

Steps to Protect

As we continue to study the ways we need to protect ourselves against Satan in our walk with Christ, let's take a quick detour through the book of Zechariah. Zechariah is one of the books in the Old Testament that gives us several helpful guidelines that we can live by. What is great about this passage found in Zechariah 7 is that it tells us what we should do, but it also comes with a warning to show us what our consequences will be if we don't do these things. Let's look at verses 8-14 to see what it is telling us:

> *⁸And the word of the Lord came again to Zechariah: ⁹This is what the Lord Almighty says: "Administer true justice; show mercy and compassion to one another; ¹⁰Do not oppress the widow or the fatherless, the alien or the poor. In your hearts do not think evil of each other."*
>
> *¹¹'But they refused to pay attention; stubbornly they*

turned their backs and stopped up their ears. ¹²They made their hearts as hard as flint and would not listen to the law or to the words that the Lord Almighty had sent by his Spirit through the earlier prophets. So the Lord Almighty was very angry.

¹³"When I called, they did not listen; so when they called, I would not listen," says the Lord Almighty. ¹⁴"I scattered them with a whirlwind among all the nations, where they were strangers. The land was left so desolate behind them that no one could come or go. This is how they made the pleasant land desolate."

We see in the first part of this passage that two of the commands that are listed mirror what Micah said in our key verse—administer justice and show mercy. God likes to repeat the points that are important. Then, as the passage concludes, I find it interesting to see how the people refused to obey and listen to the Lord. I almost want to laugh out loud when it says that the people turned their backs and stopped their ears. This is such incredibly childish behavior! A young toddler often exhibits this kind of behavior. They play Peek A Boo with their hands over their eyes as if no one could see them when their eyes were covered. These people were acting just as immature. They turned their backs on God as if He couldn't see them anymore if they turned around! Or maybe they thought if they turned around God wouldn't be there anymore. In any event, their outward behavior portrayed an outright "No!" to what God had told them.

The verses go on to say that they stopped their ears. Imagine that! It may have looked comical, but if my own children had done that to me, I would have been furious. It would have been such an extreme show of disrespect to plug their ears to what God had told them to do. I think God probably felt exactly as we would in this situation because verse 12 says that He was very angry. He had a right to be! Consequently, because of their disobedience, He said they would be scattered like a whirlwind.

As we study the Scriptures, we see that God is serious about this journey that we're on with Him. Satan knows He's serious, so he's doing the best he can to sabotage us as we try to keep living in a way that pleases God. Satan doesn't want us to show mercy and compassion to others. He doesn't want us to show true justice. And, yes, he wants us to have evil thoughts toward one another.

Now, I know that these verses are referring to the children of Israel, but we can still study these verses and learn from their mistakes. What God expected from them, He expects of us as well. Jews and Gentiles, He doesn't play favorites. If He didn't expect us to do them, then the New Testament wouldn't have included the same standards for us to live by.

Let's go ahead and take a look at what the New Testament has to say about our walk with God. After contemplating which passage would be the perfect one to end this chapter with, it was incredibly difficult to select. Should it be from Christ's words in the Gospels...who could top that? What about Paul's? Talk about a life that was changed! He certainly knew from personal experience the best way (and the worst way) that we should live our lives. But what about Peter? His epistles give us tremendous insight into our walk with God as well. How about James? It was hard, but I finally settled on a selection from Colossians that the NIV Bible entitles as "Rules for Holy Living." It's found in Colossians 3:1-17. Why don't you take a moment to read this passage.

> "*¹Since, then, you have been raised with Christ, set your hearts on things above, where Christ is seated at the right hand of God. ²Set your minds on things above, not on earthly things. ³For you died, and your life is now hidden with Christ in God. ⁴When Christ, who is your life, appears, then you also will appear with him in glory.*
>
> *⁵Put to death, therefore, whatever belongs to your earthly nature: sexual immorality, impurity, lust, evil desires and greed, which is idolatry. ⁶Because of these, the wrath of God is*

coming. ⁷You used to walk in these ways, in the life you once lived. ⁸But now you must rid yourselves of all such things as these: anger, rage, malice, slander, and filthy language from your lips. ⁹Do not lie to each other, since you have taken off your old self with its practices ¹⁰and have put on the new self, which is being renewed in knowledge in the image of its Creator. ¹¹Here there is no Greek or Jew, circumcised or uncircumcised, barbarian, Scythian, slave or free, but Christ is all, and is in all.

¹²Therefore, as God's chosen people, holy and dearly loved, clothe yourselves with compassion, kindness, humility, gentleness and patience. ¹³Bear with each other and forgive whatever grievances you may have against one another. Forgive as the Lord forgave you. ¹⁴And over all these virtues put on love, which binds them all together in perfect unity.

¹⁵Let the peace of Christ rule in your hearts, since as members of one body you were called to peace. And be thankful. ¹⁶Let the word of Christ dwell in you richly as you teach and admonish one another with all wisdom, and as you sing psalms, hymns and spiritual songs with gratitude in your hearts to God. ¹⁷And whatever you do, whether in word or deed, do it all in the name of the Lord Jesus, giving thanks to God the Father through him."

Lengthier than the Old Testament guidelines that we looked at earlier, we see that there are tremendous parallels between what we should and shouldn't do. Since we are no longer under the law but under grace, I find it interesting that our "To Do" list is even longer than the Old Testament ones that usually list only three or four commands. Once again, I believe this has to be because we would expect that we would have to do less under grace, but in actuality, we should do more.

We can find another perspective on this passage by the noted scholar, Warren W. Wiersbe. He said that "...it does little good if

Christians *declare* and *defend* the truth, but fail to *demonstrate* it in their lives…what we believe has a very definite connection with how we behave! After all, faith in Christ means being united to Christ; and if we share His life, we must follow His example. He cannot live in us by His Spirit and permit us to live in sin."

So as we defend ourselves against the wiles of the devil, it is important to have a clear understanding of this text. Let's take a look at it again. Verses 1 through 4 admonish us to set our minds and hearts on things above, not on the earthly things around us. Why don't we take a minute and write down some of the things that we should focus our minds on as we daily walk with God.

_____

_____

_____

Verses 5-6 tell us what NOT to do as a Christian. They state that we have to put our earthly nature to DEATH by getting rid of sexual immorality, impurity, lust, evil desires and greed which is idolatry. This list is self explanatory, but for someone who is new to the faith, they might think it is worded strangely. How would you reword this list to be more understandable to someone who is a new Christian? _____

_____

_____

As we continue on to verses 7-9, we see that we have to rid ourselves of anger, rage, malice, slander, and filthy language. It also mentions that we shouldn't lie. These sins don't seem as bad as the previous ones that were listed, but we have been told through teachings and through the Word of God that sin is sin. It has to be dealt with whether it is big or little. Some would argue, myself included, that the little sins are sometimes worse than the more offensive ones because they tend to be ignored. Ignored sins become unconfessed sins that will affect our relationship with God. His

Word says in Psalm 66:18 that "*If I regard iniquity in my heart, the Lord will not hear*" (NKJV). You cannot have a one-sided relationship with God, or anyone else, for that matter. A relationship or friendship takes two people working simultaneously on developing a deeper understanding of the other person. We must not let those little sins distract us on our walk with God.

Verses 10-11 tell us that we are to put on the new self. Our old self has been put away or was taken off when we accepted Christ as our Savior. We need to put on our new self to replace it. According to these verses what should our new self look like?

_____

_____

_____

Our new self should be in the image of our God, our Creator. As we continue on in this passage to verse 12, it says that we are to clothe ourselves with five specific items: compassion, kindness, humility, gentleness, and patience. Why don't you write down these five things in the order that you need to work on them in your own personal life. Notice how they are all qualities that Christ possessed as He was here on earth. _____

_____

_____

Verse 13 goes on to state that we should bear with each other and forgive any grievances that we may have against each other. The last sentence in this verse gives us a model for forgiveness. It says we are to forgive as the Lord forgave you. Write down in a few words what this means to you. _____

_____

_____

The next verse, verse 14, is what I would call an "umbrella verse." It tells us something that goes over everything else we have said so far. It is one of the final layers on this cake of commands. From this verse, we see that the ultimate covering that we must put on is love because it binds everything together in perfect unity. Love is such an important ingredient.

Verse 15 adds that we need to let God's peace rule in our hearts. We are called to peace and we should also be thankful. Usually a thankful heart *is* at peace! Continuing to verse 16, it tells us to let God's Word dwell in us richly as we teach and admonish others to sing with gratitude in their hearts to God. And lastly, verse 17 sums it all up by telling us that "...*whatever we do, whether in word or deed, do it all in the name of the Lord Jesus, giving thanks to God the Father through Him.*"

As I said before, this list we just worked through is not all inclusive. There are so many other passages that steer us, guide us, and direct us toward a deeper walk with Christ. I've listed some of these other passages at the end of this chapter so that you can study them at a more leisurely time. They're rich and yet they're simple. God doesn't want our walk with Him to be difficult to follow. Yes, the way is narrow that He has set out for us to follow, but we certainly know which path to take and how to walk along it. Praise God, He is a user friendly God offering us a life that can be the best that it can be, strengthened against the attacks of the evil one, if we walk in obedience with Him.

Other passages for further study: Ecclesiastes 12:13; Joshua 1:7-9; Deuteronomy 4:9, 6:5-9, 8:6, and 10:12-13; Ephesians 3,4, and 5; Galatians 5; and 1 Peter 1, 4.

Chapter 7

Protecting My Family Priorities

"The wise woman builds her house, but with her own hands the foolish one tears hers down" (Proverbs 14:1).

Family is important, isn't it? In the family, we learn how to love or to hate. We learn what is right and what is wrong. We learn what it means to feel safe and protected, and if we aren't, then we develop insecurities. Each of us has our own opinion of how a family should function based on our own family that we grew up with. Hopefully, your family home was a safe place to grow up in, but even if it wasn't, then we can still figure out what God expects from us in the area of family priorities. Let's take a look at some more scenarios that relate to the family unit.

Celina glared internally at her husband while outwardly her eyes smiled hopelessly. She was fed up with everything in this marriage, especially her husband. Why did he have to be so insensitive to her needs? Didn't she matter anymore? It seemed that he only could focus on one thing at a time and that was usually himself! There had to be an escape from her reality. There had to be a way out of this.

Grace stared at her children who were yelling and running 'round and 'round the couch in a full speed chase. They had completely worn her out today. They had pushed every button. And , now, she wished she were anywhere but here. She was tired and ready to call it quits to this job called "motherhood." But wait, she couldn't just tender her resignation…she could never retire from this job. There seemed to be no escape…

Hannah hung up the phone and sighed. What was she going to do? She was single and things were going great! She was having some of the best years of her life. But because she was single, it seemed that her family thought she was lonely and had nothing better to do. Rather, it was just the opposite. She had so many things on her plate that she had to say "no" all the time. She didn't want to hurt their feelings and make them feel unimportant. What was she supposed to do?

Our internal circle of family can be one of the toughest areas to deal with in our walk with God. Maybe one of these scenarios struck a familiar chord with you. Family frustrations are difficult to deal with and family bonds are hard to keep in the proper perspective. As Christians, we should have an understanding that God must be first, but, in actuality, this goes against what was ingrained in us from birth. The first thing that we could comprehend as a child was a relationship with our families. Because they were the first people that we loved and trusted before we knew anything about God, they always seemed to edge into the boundaries of our first priority toward God.

Satan knows how we struggle in this area. Family ties are hard to be broken. Yet at the same time, family feuds devastate and divide the closest family circles. It is so true that many times we act the worst within the comforts of our own homes around people we are supposed to love. Satan jumps on this. For anything that Satan can do to tear our family units down, is his next plan of attack against us. He's aware of the power plays involved with family and is set to undermine all of our attempts to have a godly relationship with those we love.

If we know Satan is going to behave this way, then why do we have so much trouble with him? We're privy to his attack so we are able to set up our defenses before he confronts us in the battle for our families. Too often, though, we are just plain lazy and don't want to make a constant effort to fortify our families. We let our guard down with the false assumption that our family relationships will be okay even if we don't consciously focus on our family every second of every day. I don't know about you, but as for me, if I'm not continuously focused on protecting my family in the world that we live in, then I will get sabotaged by Satan. It's subtle, oh yes! But he is after every single opportunity to tear us apart and disintegrate us from within.

That's why God's plan for families is so important. Genesis 2:23-24 tells of God's plan for families from the beginning of time.

> *"The man said, 'This is now bone of my bones and flesh of my flesh; she shall be called "woman," for she was taken out of man.' For this reason a man will leave his father and mother and be united to his wife, and they will become one flesh."*

These verses tell us that when God instituted marriage, He desired that a man would leave his father and mother and cleave (or be united) to his wife. He had a set course of action for the family unit from the very beginning.

God did not stop in Genesis with the admonishments to the husband and the wife. He also told fathers not to exasperate their children, but train them up in the Lord in Ephesians 6:4. Throughout the Proverbs, we see that parents are supposed to teach their children what is right. Ephesians 6 tells children that they are to honor and obey their parents. Chapter 5 of Ephesians gives some additional instruction to the husband and wife. This chapter tells husbands that they are to love their wives as Christ loved the church and wives are to submit to their husbands as the church submits to Christ. It also says that a man nourishes and cherishes his own flesh (or family) just as the Lord nourishes and cherishes the church.

God's Word sounds simple and clear cut. But have you ever stopped and pondered why God's Word can sound so easy to follow, yet be so hard, all at the same time? I have! For instance, in the area of our priorities, God clearly states in Isaiah 45:18 that, "He is the Lord, there is no other." Solomon even summed it up succinctly, in Ecclesiastes 12:13, by stating that all we need to do is "Fear God and keep His commandments." With God first, then family would fall next in line. But, somehow, even with these clear messages from Scripture, we tend to complicate our lives by letting our guard down and allowing Satan to get a stronghold. Why do we do that? How come we have to make things so difficult for ourselves?

There's a wonderful parallel to our own lives that we can make from Acts 1:8. Jesus declares in His last words to His disciples that *"...you will receive power when the Holy Spirit comes on you; and you will be my witnesses in Jerusalem, and in all Judea and Samaria, and to the ends of the earth."*

If we can grasp what Christ is saying in the area of spreading the Gospel, we can use the same game plan for our own lives. This verse is a proven model for missions. It starts at home and then reaches to the ends of the earth. God's plan of protection for our lives works much the same way. It models a life centered on a personal relationship with God and extends to the work place and outside ministries.

Let's think about this a little bit more. Which people are we supposed to reach out to after we put God first? Acts 1:8 gives us a map of how we are to be an effective witness for Christ. But what if we took this same principle of "starting from within" and then "moving outward" from our circle of influence and applied it to our priorities? We can use Acts 1:8 as a guide for our priorities because it gives us a visual of how we are to accomplish this task of being an effective witness for Christ.

Let's look a little closer at Acts 1:8 in order to get a better understanding of this. This verse tells us that we are to witness in our immediate vicinity, then start spreading out into the surrounding areas, eventually ending with us reaching out to the world. You see, if we compare this to our daily lives, then our Jerusalem is parallel to our relationship with God. Judea is parallel to our home with our husbands, children, etc. Samaria is parallel to our work and/or our ministries. And then the ends of the earth are all the other things that fall into our priorities after them. Here's a visual model of what that would look like:

ACTS 1:8 -- A Literal Representation of the Verse

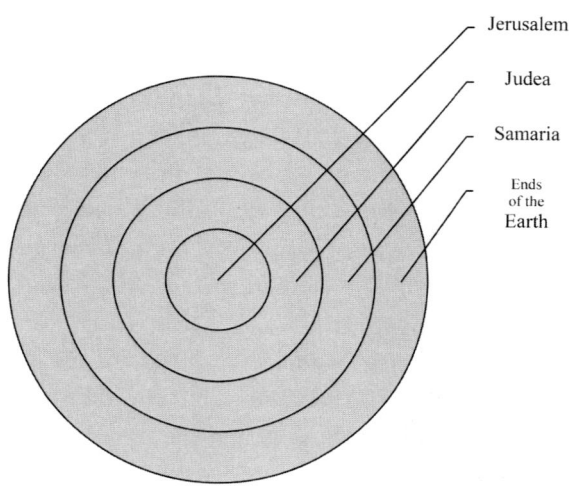

ACTS 1:8 -- A Parallel To The Areas We Must Protect

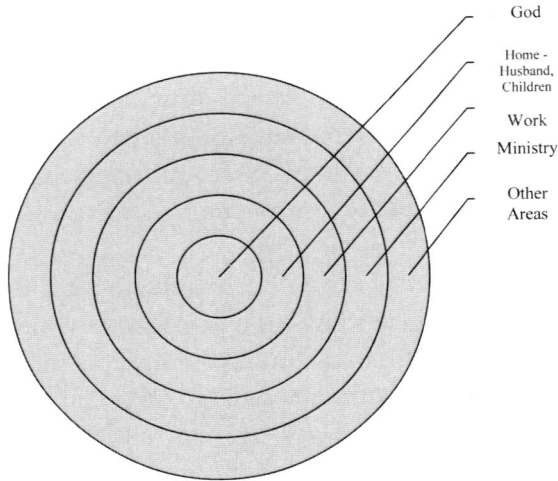

With this unique parallel to Scripture, we can clearly see, with God as our center, that our next area of focus should be to our immediate family. So, as we turn our attention to them, we will investigate how we can protect our relationships with our husbands (if we're married), our children, and our immediate family (if single). Remember, Satan knows this can be tricky territory, so let's not let him get control.

This reminds me of a story from the Old Testament about a woman who knew what God expected of her and who tried to live her life accordingly. This woman kept her priorities in order, and because she was obedient in this area, God blessed her for it. To illustrate this point, why don't you take a short journey with me as we look at this incredible woman from God's Word.

Hannah looked outside her window. The day was bright and beckoning and there was a timid breeze drifting through the air. As she watched the leaves wave gently to each other, she longed to join them in their outdoor salute. A fresh drink from the well would be a welcome reprieve for her parched throat. Yet she hesitated to go outdoors. There were children playing by the well so she knew that Peninnah, their mother, would be nearby. Peninnah was always ready to say an unkind word to Hannah.

Hannah hated negativity and confrontation. Why, oh why, did Peninnah always taunt her about her barrenness and make her feel so insignificant? It wasn't like she could change her childless state by simply willing it to be so. So she resolved to the fact that she was destined to be barren until the time God chose to open up her womb. There was absolutely nothing that she could do about it, except fret. And she really tried not to. She would rather ponder the things that made her happy.

"I guess I'll wait to get a drink at another time. I just can't bear the thought of being belittled again by that woman!" Hannah thought.

So she turned from the window and began her housework encompassed with the thoughts of how she didn't measure up.

And so it was, year after year. Her attempts at humor and a positive outlook were constantly dashed by the brutal words of Peninnah. It seemed that the more she tried to be positive and ignore Peninnah's remarks, the deeper into the pit of despond she fell. Each time she fell in, it became harder and harder to climb out.

"It is no use!" she wept bitterly, "my life is empty of children, so I have no reason to be happy. I will never make my husband proud to have a son."

But what Hannah failed to notice, was her husband's devotion to her, whether she had children or not. Each year at the time of sacrifice, he would give her a double portion to give to the priests. He was trying to show her that her childless state did not change his feelings for her. He only wished that he could soothe her soul and help her to know that he was not bothered by the things that she was.

As the time for sacrifice came again, Hannah resolved that she would speak to the Lord about her situation. She was tired of living this way. She knew that there was nothing that she could do, but an Almighty God could do anything. Right? Perhaps He would look favorably in her direction.

After dinner in Shiloh, where they had come to sacrifice, she slipped out and made her way to the tabernacle. As she neared the holy structure, she felt her heaviness of heart grow bigger and bigger. So great was her grief that she fell to her knees and wept bitterly to the Lord.

"O Lord, look into my heart and see my pain!" she silently cried out as her mouth was moving. "Remember your maidservant desires a child. Not just any child, Lord, but a child that I could give back to You."

The Lord heard Hannah's request and blessed her with a boy that would some day grow up to be one of the greatest prophets in Israel's history. His name was Samuel.

Hannah's life was a fairly difficult one. By today's standards, we would have to say that she was verbally abused on a regular basis. This abuse went on for years and years, and Hannah bore it all. The implications of what she went through makes me shudder as a fellow wife and mother. To endure such taunting day in and day out shows the strength of her character. Yes, she had her "down" days, because the Bible says that she wept bitterly and did not eat in 1 Samuel 1:7. This allowed her human side to come forward. Yet, what is interesting, is that she did not lash out in any other ways in our passage. Today, women would applaud her outbursts as justifiable, if she had made any. Any negative behaviors would have been excused, if she had exhibited any. But in the midst of her physical and mental suffering, she never fell to those extremes. As we look at this passage in 1 Samuel 1 and 2, there are several admirable behaviors that she displayed.

First, she never retaliated against Peninnah. Secondly, she kept her problems out of the public. Her problems did not need to become someone else's. And thirdly, she never cursed or denied the Lord.

These are some pretty admirable traits for someone who had borne so much grief in her life. But we see here that Hannah had made a choice. Instead of taking the low road, she had chosen to take the high road. She knew that she had to keep her priorities straight in order for God to bless her. She did not need to complain to others. She only needed to lay her burdens down at the feet of her Jehovah. He would bless her according to His tender mercies.

Hannah was right. God did bless her humble spirit and her heart that desired to do the right thing. He blessed her because she knew where to come in the time of trouble—straight to the Lord—instead of trying to solve her problems on her own. Hannah had her priorities straight. She knew that God must come first, and that her family must come second.

Just as Hannah took steps to keep her own priorities in order, we need to take steps to protect our priorities as well. After putting God first, we have to realize that Satan is definitely going to come and attack our priority number two—our families. So join with me as we take some steps to protect these family areas in our lives from the sneaky and subtle grasp of Satan.

Our Priorities to Our Husbands

As I think about being married, I find myself viewing it as a growing, evolving relationship. It is similar to our relationship with God. In our spiritual lives, we start out as babies that know next to nothing. But as we study God's Word, we mature and become more and more Christ-like. In a marriage, we also start out as babies with so much to learn and so much ahead of us to experience. Often times, though, what began as something new and exciting often becomes something that is very familiar and comfortable. Now familiar and comfortable are good things—but if we are not careful, then it can become mundane and boring. This familiarity can cause all sorts of marital dilemmas if we don't recognize the problem signs as they come and set things straight.

As a teacher, I know that the best way to learn about something is to give examples—whether visual, hands-on, or kinesthetic. So that is exactly what I am going to do here. We already know that Satan wants to keep us from being a godly wife. So how do we counteract against his attacks? The best way is to figure out what we are up against and then, as the armed services call it, take some "countermeasures." So let's take a look at three examples of how a wife responds in a marriage and determine which example is the one we should be following. Hopefully, this will help us to understand what God expects from us as wives so that we can protect our marriage relationship from Satan's attacks.

Example 1: The "If I Feel Like It" Wife

The first example of marriage is the one I like to label as "If I Feel Like It." Do you know those couples that have an "if I feel like it" relationship? I'm sure you do. They are the couples that have one spouse that is totally sold out to a cause and one that is completely uninterested. Because of their lack of interest in doing things as a team, it is inevitable for them to excuse their behavior because they "don't feel like it." Now, it is perfectly alright for couples to have separate interests, I'm not trying to start an argument here! But couples who are in tune with the Lord and in tune with each other know the boundaries lines of personal involvement. But they also know what God expects from their relationship, too. They will use the principle of "Going the Extra Mile" found in Matthew 5:41 which says, *And whoever compels you to go one mile, go with him two*" (NKJV). They won't be concentrating on doing the bare minimum in their relationship, but instead, will strive for the maximum effort in all that they do.

The primary problem with this whole mind set of "If I Feel Like It" is that it is steeped in failure. I mean really. Look at the two main words in that statement. "If" and "Feel." Neither one of those words promote any kind of certainty or assurance in ANYTHING. "If" is just another word for "maybe" or "perhaps." And "Feel," well, we know how feelings can change, especially as women. The time of day, the time of month, or even the season of the year can affect that one. Both words leave us with an unsettled feeling down in the pit of our stomach, so just think of how they affect a marriage relationship. The "If I Feel Like It" wife is one who:

- Will help her husband, IF she's not too busy.

- Will make dinner, IF she's not too tired.

- Will put her husband's needs ahead of hers, IF it makes her look good.

- Will bend over backwards for her husband, IF she feels like it!

Imagine this relationship. With a wife like this, what can a husband depend on? Absolutely nothing! Maybe she will or maybe she won't—the husband hesitates to ask or get involved. This unsettled feeling is disturbing to a husband because it reminds him of when he was single and dating. Would she say "yes" to him when he asked her to go to dinner or would she say "no"? Would she take his calls or wouldn't she? Would she find him attractive and pleasant and be proud to be around him? Or would she be disgusted with what she saw in him? Men hate to play those mind games and they will immediately put up defenses against them. They had to play them before they got married, they certainly DON'T want to play them again!

As wives, we have to watch our attitudes because our husbands can read them fairly well. So what should a wife's attitude reflect? This question reminds me of a verse that shows the Lord's attitude toward us. It's found in 2 Peter 3:8-9. It states,

> *"But do not forget this one thing, dear friends: With the Lord a day is like a thousand years, and a thousand years are like a day.* **The Lord is not slow in keeping his promise,** *as some understand slowness. He is patient with you, not wanting anyone to perish, but everyone to come to repentance."*

The Lord is not slow, or slack, as some versions say, in His relationship with us. He can be counted on each and every time we need Him. He will always be there for us. This is exactly how we should be for our husbands as well. Whether we like it or not, we need to be there. When we can't consistently help our spouse, do our responsibilities in the marriage relationship, and make our husband feel like he is treasured and loved, we become someone that cannot be relied on in our husband's eyes.

When we will only do things IF we feel like it, then we are losing an essential element of trust with our husbands. He needs to know that he can count on us to help him every single time. He shouldn't have to wonder whether or not we will be available for him. Why is this so important? Because each time he sees that he can depend on us, it shows that we care about him. By doing so, we are putting a building block on our relationship that will eventually become a strong defense against the attacks of Satan that will come. This is how we start to build a solid foundation with our mates. Don't be an "iffy" person. Being "iffy" may sound like a good choice at times when we are feeling selfish, but it is no where close to being the better or best choice.

Example 2: The 50/50 Wife

The next example involves the wife that is sold out to the 50/50 Rule. Now, before you start judging, 50/50 is quite a nifty number. Fifty/fifty can be a great thing! When you're going to a movie and dinner with a friend, it's certainly more cost effective for you to split the bill 50/50. When you are doing a project, you can divide the research and work 50/50 so there is not a huge burden on just one person. Also, 50/50 can be a great time saver and a huge burden lifter. But how does it work in a marriage? You probably already know that it doesn't.

The 50/50 wife is the one who will always meet you half way. You can count on her to be there, just not with everything fiber of her being. You probably know wives like this and so do I. In fact, I sometimes see this person in my own mirror at home. (How'd she get in there?) This person is always willing to help out but she wants to make sure that her husband is helping, too. And may I add, he'd better be helping just as much as she is!

Working full time as a school teacher, teaching ladies Bible classes, writing, and being a pastor's wife on top of being a wife and mother can be extremely difficult sometimes! When I get bogged down with all my responsibilities, I find myself slipping into this 50/50 attitude. I have to remind myself, when I feel myself falling, that when I am standing before my God in heaven I will only be accountable for my own actions, not the actions of my husband. This motivates me to make sure that no matter what is happening around me, I must choose to do the right thing.

Matthew 6:24 and Luke 16:13 lend an important perspective to the 50/50 marriage situation. These verses say,

"No one can serve two masters. Either he will hate the one and love the other, or he will be devoted to the one and despise the other. You cannot serve both God and money."

Now I know we are talking about our husbands and not money, but the principle in this verse applies so well to our illustration. Let's look at the very first phrase in this verse. It says that no one can serve two masters. In essence, you cannot surrender everything to two different things. As humans we weren't made that way. We can only give our all to one thing at a time, otherwise, we have to divide our attention.

Back in Jesus' time, the Pharisees thought that "devotion to money and devotion to God were perfectly compatible. This went hand in hand with the commonly held notion that earthly riches signifies divine blessing," according to John MacArthur. Jesus had to dispel this teaching by giving them a clear choice. They either loved God or they loved money. Loving money was not a substitute to loving God.

When we have a 50/50 relationship in a marriage, we are equally focused on our husband (not necessarily a bad thing) and ourselves (not necessarily a good thing). We already know God's stance—it will not work! Why? Because equal attention means there is a lack of excellence in both areas. Neither one is given the attention they need or deserve. Consequently, an unhealthy relationship begins to develop. Being a 50/50 wife is certainly a better choice than the "If I Feel Like It" wife, but it is still not the best choice to make in a marriage.

Example 3: The "All or Nothing" Wife

The third and proper example is what we would call the all or nothing wife. This is the wife who gives it her all—100%—and if she can't, she won't even get involved. This wife made a commitment to her husband and is sticking to it until death do us part. This is the kind of woman that you can count on to do an excellent job every time she is asked to do something. You might even call her "Superwoman."

We saw with our earlier example that being fifty/fifty isn't Scriptural because you cannot serve two masters. In this example, we see that this kind of wife focuses all her attention on taking care of and loving her husband. This wife said "I Do" on her wedding day and will fulfill her promise as long as she is living and able. But what does Scripture say about this? God's Word is very clear about commitments. So let's look at some verses together and figure out what God has to tell us.

"Simply let your 'Yes' be 'Yes,' and your 'No,' 'No'; anything beyond this comes from the evil one" (Matthew 5:37).

"Above all, my brothers, do not swear—not by heaven or by earth or by anything else. Let your "Yes" be yes, and your "No," no, or you will be condemned" (James 5:12).

James is echoing the Gospels when it says that we should let our "yes" mean "yes" and our "no" mean "no." God is serious about commitments. He wants us to be women of our word. He doesn't want our testimony to be one that is uncertain or difficult to read by others. Instead, He would rather people knew exactly who we are and that we mean what we say when we speak to them. After all, we are His ambassadors (2 Corinthians 5:20) and God desires the best of the best.

Finally, we see in another verse, 1 Corinthians 7:17, that God has commanded us to make the best of things. This is what it says.

"Nevertheless, each one should retain the place in life that the Lord assigned to him and to which God has called him. This is the rule I lay down in all the churches."

Wycliffe gives a great explanation of this verse in his commentary. It says, "The apostle (Paul) now summarizes, indicating that this principle of abiding in one's marital relationship is simply part of a more general principle touching every sphere of life. The rule in everything is to abide in one's calling unless that calling be immoral."

So let me explain why I chose to end with this verse and why I included it here. There is a widespread phenomenon in our society of walking away from responsibility. In this age of the new "truth" that is in the secular world, people have begun to excuse their behaviors. Even behaviors which would have been labeled as "laziness," "incompetence," and "lack of perseverance" years ago are now being excused as "bored," "misplaced," and "unchallenged." The moral decline in our world as we know it is affecting our interpretation of truth. As people are reading their Bibles, they are putting more self-interpretation into it instead of relying on proven Bible study techniques. We must be very careful to not put our own "spin" on something that we read.

As we look at the meaning of our verse in 1 Corinthians 7:17, we need to take away this truth. Wherever God has placed you, you need to give it your best. You need to work as if God was standing right beside you and is going to give you a grade on your efforts. You also need to be content where He has called you. If you are married, you are called to be the best wife ever for your mate.

Satan does not want us to believe that. Satan wants us to take our focus off of our priorities and direct them on ourselves. He knows we are selfish creatures and that it will not take much effort to accomplish his tricks. Satan does not want us to remain in a committed and happy relationship with our spouse. No, he wants us to struggle to the point that we want out of it. While our verses reinforce commitment and self-denial, the media and our society portray just the opposite as being the truth. They brainwash us to take care of ourselves first because we are "special." They want us to change our focus to one that selfishly looks inside before it will look outside. So don't get sidetracked with what the world tries to tell you. Protecting your marriage is the absolute best choice that you can make for your family.

Our Priorities to Our Children

Children are such a blessing to the family unit and provide many unique opportunities for us to share the gift of Jesus Christ. Yet with most things, the positives sometimes come with negatives. Imagine that! It is possible that our focus on our children will lead to an oversight of God as we get distracted and fall into the world's ways of thinking. Let me explain—because I am certainly not saying that children cause us to live sinful lives and put us on a downward spiral towards family ruin. It's just that in our zest to be the best parent we can possibly be, we can be easily swayed into parenting as the world teaches. We forget about what God's Word says on the subject because the society norms for new parents make sense at first glance.

For instance, it seems reasonable to talk things out or explain a situation instead of expecting immediate obedience from our children. After all, we don't want to appear to be uncaring or inattentive. However, when we always do as the world suggests, we are sending the message to our children that the discussion is more important than the obedience and that they are allowed to verbally disagree with our decision. An explanation is always nice, but obedience should be the expected outcome whether our "reasonings" make sense or not to our children. Oftentimes, these discussions lead to arguments that could easily be avoided. Kids do not need to know every reason we expect something. What are we teaching them by doing this? If they questioned everything their boss did at work, would they be employed for long? Sometimes the simple, "Because I told you so," is best. It teaches them respect for authority.

The world also tells us that we should trust our children. Let kids be kids. It is okay for them to experiment because you have to "live and learn." Learning from our mistakes sounds good at first because that's how most of us learned. But without intervention, we are sending our children to the wolves with this philosophy. Instead of investing in some personal training about the dangers that lurk in a life that is not fully devoted to Christ, we are allowing them to get a taste of the sin. Then, when they detour off of the right path, we try to reel them back in when we see that they are starting to make a mess of their own lives.

We need some intervention here! There is absolutely nothing wrong with sheltering your children from the dangers that Satan has for them. If we will not protect our own children, then who will? School teachers don't know your moral code at home. Most are tongue-tied by their school boards and school districts from guiding your child's moral compass. And as a fellow teacher myself, when I look around at my peers in my field, I am shocked by the lack of morality in the leaders of the classrooms. We should never trust someone else to do our job as a parent. Other adults in our children's lives don't have ownership in them like we do and are apt to only give it a half-hearted effort.

God loves children and continually recognizes them in His heavenly plan. He told Abraham in Genesis, one of His blessings was that he would be fruitful and multiply—his descendants would be more than the stars in the sky and the sand along the sea. In Bible times, children signified wealth, achievement, and abundance. Having many children was considered reputable and admirable and, according to Psalms, they were a heritage and a reward. Today we might joke about someone with a lot of children and say that maybe they need a TV or a hobby. Quantity has a negative connotation in today's world. However, back in the Bible times, it was exactly the opposite. No matter what the viewpoint, God's Word has many definite things to say about children. Here is one example in Psalm 127:3-5a. It says,

> *"Sons are a heritage from the LORD, children a reward from him. Like arrows in the hands of a warrior are sons born in one's youth. Blessed is the man whose   quiver is full of them."*

God loves little children, there's no denying that. In the Gospels, He even told His disciples to let the little children come to Him. The disciples thought that they might distract or bother Jesus, but it was quite the opposite. He enjoyed them and loved them. But what about us as parents? How are we supposed to act toward and protect our children? What is our role as mothers as we try to make the best choices in child-rearing? As always, God's

Word holds all the answers we need.

I'd like for us to look at an example in Scripture that will help us to parent the way God would want us to. This Scripture is found in Deuteronomy 6:4-9 and says,

"Hear O Israel: The Lord our God, the Lord is one. Love the Lord with all your heart and with all your soul and with all your strength. These commandments that I give you today are to be upon your hearts. Impress them on your children. Talk about them when you sit at home and when you walk along the road, when you lie down and when you get up. Tie them as symbols on your hand and bind them on your foreheads. Write them on the door frames of you houses and on your gates."

What an important passage from God's Word! God recognized that parents needed help in raising their children, so He included some instructions in His Holy Scriptures that were directly for our benefit. Being a parent is a hard job. Even if we think we know all the answers, there will be some point in time as we are parenting that we will not know what to do. But if we have an understanding of the principles from this passage in Deuteronomy, then we can at least be assured that we are on the right track. According to Reggie Joiner, here are some applications from Deuteronomy 6 that he came up with to explain what the family leader should transfer to their children.

1. Relationship comes before rules. v. 5

2. Truth must be in you before it can be in them. v. 6

3. Each day offers natural opportunities for teaching. v. 7
    a. When you sit at home: meal time
    b. When you walk along the road: drive time
    c. When you lie down: bedtime
    d. When you get up: get-ready time

4. Repetition is the teacher's best friend. v. 8, 9

This list encompasses every time frame that we have with our children during the day. Parenting is not something that we can set aside and come back to when it's convenient. It takes constant work and continual protection. It is a job that takes twenty-four hours of every day for a minimum of eighteen years.

I don't know about you, but parenting has been the hardest job I have ever had. Sometimes I wonder if I had known how hard it was going to be, would I have still become a mother? Maybe it's a good thing I didn't know! But the answer to my question is probably "Yes!" It is a natural desire for us to procreate. I can tell you this one thing for sure, though, since I have become a parent, I have learned a whole lot about myself. In trying to be the person and the parent that God wants me to be, I have had to struggle with pride and selfishness on a regular basis. If you find yourself struggling with this, too, please know that you are not the only one that has ever felt this way. I battle this all of the time.

"Never Say Never" Parenting

As we try to raise our children, there are three basic approaches that we can take. The first approach is one that I like to call "Never Say Never." Now really, is there ever a human being who is just a natural at child rearing and has all the answers without ever getting any type of training? No. Everyone has had some sort of training, even if it was only mental notes of what they had observed that they liked or disliked about how their parents raised them.

As Christians, we need to be aware of the "Never Say Never" falsehood that is being propagated and take measures to protect our own homes from its subtle strongholds. What do we need to look out for in order to protect ourselves from this? We need to beware of phrases like "Don't ever say 'no' to your child because it will have a negative impact on them," "Don't discipline your children," "Don't place boundaries around your child." Instead, the world would say, "Let your child experiment with things" and "Let trial and error be your guide." The world that we live in would say that all of these negative types of "Don't" phrases would severely hinder their mental and physical development. For instance, you might have heard this worldly comment that if you have a genius for a child and you restrain him, then he will never reach his new potential. You may have also heard, "He needs to be free to experiment; therefore, never use restraint." This is all a bunch of baloney. What genius do you know that would be trapped by his or her circumstances? None. People with incredible gifts usually find a way to express and use them. Nothing ever seems to stop them. A simple word like "never" or "no" cannot change the IQ and potential of a human being.

Society has bought into Satan's way of thinking. They think that all we have to do is keep emphasizing the positive, but, as Christians, we know that this is not true. Take fire for instance. Fire can be very beneficial and useful. It can also be very cozy as you gather around a campfire. But this same fire with all of its positive qualities can quickly become deadly and destructive. It is a negative thing as well as positive. If we do not warn of the dangers in life, then our loved ones will eventually get hurt. It is our duty to impart the good and the bad as we rear our children. It is okay to tell them "no" because in so doing, you may be protecting or saving their life.

The type of child who is raised in the "Never Say Never" fashion will eventually become unruly and undisciplined. When a young child is never told "no" or "don't do that," they begin to believe that they are invincible and that everything is permissible to them. Consequently, their behavior begins to follow the behaviors of sinful man because, unchecked, a person's life will go the direction of doing whatever they feel like doing. Only when boundaries are put in place can a person start to understand the difference between right and wrong.

No parent intentionally wants to raise a child to be this way. Life is miserable when we have to live day in and day out with children like this. What does God say about these kinds of children? Here are two verses to help us understand how strongly God views this type of child and how serious an issue this can become.

"Woe to the obstinate children," declares the LORD, "to those who carry out plans that are not mine, forming an alliance, but not by my Spirit, heaping sin upon sin" (Isaiah 30:1).

"If you are not disciplined (and everyone undergoes discipline), then you are illegitimate children and not true sons" (Hebrews 12:8).

The main problem with this "Never Say Never" parenting style is that we are not teaching our children how to make good choices. Instead of worrying about the emotional effects of "no" on our children, we should be more concerned about teaching them how to protect themselves, and not permitting them to stumble right into the traps of Satan.

It is interesting how a child raised this way will begin to exhibit certain behaviors. I have noticed these behaviors in the classroom as a teacher and in our middle schools and high schools as I work with the youth in my hometown. Young people that were raised with this "Never say Never" mentality will not listen to authority because they have always been their own authority. They will tend to put self ahead of others because life has always been about pleasing them. They will not be good at following directions because they are not used to being told what to do. Because they have not been steered in the right direction and have not experienced the distinct consequences of right and wrong behavior, they lack a moral, internal guidance system that most of us depend on as we make important decisions in life. They will be the child that is rebellious, rude, and self-centered.

The warning signs are out there. Unfortunately, not many people are paying attention to them. Only with God's help can we face this battle with Satan head on. He is the only One who can lead us down the right path if we will just let Him.

"Like It or Lump It" Parenting

The next approach that many parents have with their children is one called "Like It or Lump It." This way of parenting is just the opposite of the previous one mentioned. This parent is always concerned that their child may do something wrong and so they go to the opposite extreme to make sure that doesn't happen.

The problem with this parenting style is that it never allows the child to be free to express their obedience. They are always made to obey; therefore, they can never show their mom or dad that obedience would have been the choice they would have taken without parental intervention. As the previous style was focused on "Never Say Never," this one is consumed with "Always Do As I Say" and if you don't like it, then too bad. Neither one is the proper attitude.

A parent who follows the "Like It or Lump It" philosophy will eventually frustrate their children. Over time, they will get consumed with anger at never being able to express themselves and always being told what to do. This child will usually end up in rebellion because they just cannot stand it anymore. Here's what God says about these kinds of parents and children:

> *"Fathers, do not exasperate your children; instead, bring them up in the training and instruction of the Lord"* (Ephesians 6:4).

> *"Fathers, do not embitter your children, or they will become discouraged"* (Colossians 3:21).

According to these verses from God's Word, the parent can be the problem! It is not always the child's fault. We have to be careful that we don't cause our children to get discouraged. Now this is a somewhat silly example that I am going to make on this point, but I remember when I was a young girl and my responsibilities at home included the chore of emptying the dishwasher. I would hate it when my mother would tell me to put away the dishes because I always wanted to get it done before she would say something. Now, in all honesty, I was not in trouble for anything that I had done or didn't do. I was just given a friendly reminder. However, I remember getting so discouraged when the subject of putting the dishes away came up because I felt that it implied that I was being irresponsible.

As we look back at Ephesians, we see that it tells us that we are able to exasperate our children. What exactly does exasperate mean? It means to irritate or aggravate or excite to anger (cause to get angry) according to Merriam-Webster. Just like our own children can sometimes cause us to get exasperated, we can also cause this feeling in them. We are the grown up in the situation so we need to be careful that we are not causing our child to sin because of something we are doing. Since God says it in His Word, we will be held accountable for our parental behaviors as well.

Unfortunately the child raised in the "Like It or Lump It" fashion will not be able to think for themselves when they become a grown up. This type of child tends to become dependent instead of independent. As a parent myself, I know my responsibility is to teach my three children to someday become independent of me and the family unit they have been surrounded with their entire lives. I also don't want them to get so defiant towards authority, that they grow up without a natural respect for the authority that is placed in their lives. They need to know how to survive and make wise decisions all on their own without any of my help. They need to learn how to function in society so that someday they can make this world a better place. When we force feed them every action that they are going to take, then we are doing them a disservice. Instead of protecting them from Satan's evils, we are frustrating them and perhaps angering them to a point of rebellion. "Like It or Lump It" is not the course of action we should take.

"Relationship with Rules" Parenting

The last approach is the type of parenting that produces the most favorable results. This style of "Relationship with Rules" is one that emphasizes a loving relationship with your children but is clearly defined by boundaries and rules. If Jesus had been an earthly parent, this would be the style He would have used. He lived His life on earth teaching the mysteries and practicalities of God. He did so in a way that made sense to those around Him because He used visuals and stories to teach His points. He also taught by example and personally demonstrated many of the areas He was emphasizing. He was an incredible teacher because of this. Our parenting style should replicate His methods.

Having a "Relationship with Rules" is all of the positives from the other methods rolled into one—and then some. Parents mistakenly think that they are building a relationship with their children in the "Never Say Never" style because they are always encouraging their children. However, they really aren't encouraging them when they are setting them up for failure *later* in life, are they? The "Like It or Lump It" method is way too strict and discouraging and doesn't appear reasonable to most children, therefore, they again are set up for failure because they become frustrated *early* in life. This last style is a healthy mix of the two and includes guiding, reasoning, and instructing. This is the best way to build a relationship with your child. When they see that you are putting in a conscious and continuous effort, their respect for you as a parent increases. And as they see your consistency, their behavior reflects their respect.

This style involves teaching God's Word and following it by both the child and the parent. Let's take a look and see what the Bible tells us to do. According to Ephesians 6:1, it says, "*Children, obey your parents in the Lord, for this is right.*" Children have a responsibility to obey according to this verse. But parents also have some guidelines, too. Let's look at what Psalm 78:5-7 says,

> *"He decreed statutes for Jacob and established the law in Israel, which he commanded our forefathers to teach their children, so the next generation would know them, even the children yet to be born, and they in turn would tell their children. Then they would put their trust in God and would not forget his deeds but would keep his commands."*

The parent is responsible for teaching God's laws to their children so that they can pass them down to future generations. A good parent leaves a legacy behind and knows how to give good gifts to their children (Matthew 7:11). They also know that children need this discipline and protection in their lives and that discipline will make them behave according to the basic moral code of society so that they and their future children will become a crown and a glory to the parents and grandparents (Proverbs 17:6). When you take time and invest it into your children along with the truth and guidance from Scripture, you will never go wrong. You will have a "Relationship with Rules" with your children.

Our Priority of Singleness

I want to close this chapter on family priorities with a word to those of you who are single. It can be extremely difficult to be single in our world today because we lack an accountability partner in the home that will keep tabs on us. And since we live alone, we feel, at times, more obligated to our immediate and extended family. It's hard to balance life when we don't know how much is too much or how little is too little.

But just as a wife knows that her family priorities must go first to her husband and then to her children, our priorities as single women must be our relationship with God. When we are of age, we don't have to answer to our parents anymore. Respect and honor them, yes, according to Ephesians 6:1-3, but obey their every request as an adult? No. God needs to be our filter here because singleness can pose its own set of complications with our family priorities. God will let us know how much or how little we should include family as we strive to live our lives for Him.

Our families can make us feel pretty guilty about some decisions that seem to exclude them. Many family members will feel the "need" to constantly add their two cents even when it is not solicited. Don't be discouraged, though, because God's Word specifically speaks to ladies just like us. In 1 Corinthians 7: 8 Paul says,

"Now to the unmarried and the widows I say: It is good for them to stay unmarried, as I am."

Paul knew the struggles of being married, so he was advocating singleness! So many times we try to turn this around and think "poor me, I don't have anyone in my life." But Paul was praising the single position! The world and Satan would like us to think that we are strange or different if we don't have a special someone in our life. That we are only complete if we have a partner. Paul is saying exactly the opposite. We are complete if we are single. Our only focus and partner is Jesus Christ. The fact is we are going to have struggles if we are married because our focus turns to a person rather than the Savior.

For many singles, their faith is tested at every bend in the road. When faced with a choice, it is always important to remember that God will bless obedience to Him. Knowing that singles will someday be rewarded for their faithfulness does not always make up for being alone. We have to stay faithful, though. Hang on! Satan knows the mind games that are out there and he is ready to play a few of them. So stand strong and accept this position that God has given us in life with pride. God has us exactly where

He wants us if we are single and we have to trust Him with His plans for us.

Steps to Protect

As we sum up this chapter, we have already been given many steps to protect ourselves from Satan's grasp. But we would be wise to remember as this lesson draws to a close, the admonition that Solomon gave us which was chosen as this chapter's key verse. It says:

"The wise woman builds her house, but with her own hands the foolish one tears hers down" (Proverbs 14:1).

We have a simple choice as women. We can either build up our house or we can tear it down. If we keep our priorities in order and follow God's guidelines, then we will be considered wise, like the verse says. But if we try to do things our own way, then all our attempts will result in foolishness.

When all is said and done in this life, I want to be known as a wise woman, don't you? What an honor to be known as a godly woman that lived her life according to God's plan. His plan is simple and straightforward. It is our sinful nature that listens to Satan's lies which begins to complicate things for us.

So remember what God said in His Word—*"we have been given everything we need that pertains to life and godliness."* So let's not lose sight of the goal. Let's keep Satan at a distance, keep God's Word in our hearts, and keep our family priorities in their God-designed order.

Chapter 8

Protecting my Career
and Calling

"Therefore, my dear brothers, stand firm. Let nothing move you. Always give yourselves fully to the work of the Lord, because you know that your labor in the Lord is not in vain" (1 Corinthians 15:58).

Work. To some this word is like fingernails going across a chalkboard and is in the same category as other negative, four letter words. They feel resentment at being there, they don't enjoy their job, or they just feel "stuck" with nowhere else to go. But to others, work elicits only happy, pleasant thoughts. They can't wait to get there every day because they love their job. Maybe their job fulfills the need for income but also allows them to do ministry as well. Or they are bored at home. Take the following scenario, for instance.

Chris couldn't wait to get to her desk. She had figured out the answer to her problem with payroll yesterday afternoon. In the middle of the night it had come to her. She must have posted the wrong time which would explain her discrepancy in the number of hours worked on her coworker's time card.

But as she rounded the corner near her desk, she noticed that Liz's spot was empty. This was a common occurrence and shouldn't have caught her eye as being abnormal, but somehow, she noticed her absence today. Why hadn't she observed this before? She loved her job and couldn't wait to get there each morning. The challenges were exciting and she had never learned so much in her life! Each day was a new adventure. Didn't Liz feel the same way? Apparently not. For as soon as she thought it, Liz came around the corner, too, with a frown spread all over her face. It seemed to scream out in bitterness to all those who saw her, "Liz was not happy to be here."

Such a varied response to just one little word called "Work"! Why are there such different extremes to this daily ritual that most of us engage in? For most of us, it can be summed up with yet another word—"perspective." It is our perspective that affects our response to work. And we will find that our perspective is altered by how we were raised, what our circumstances are, and what we know of what the Bible says.

Take me for instance. I was raised to believe that the Bible said that a woman should be at home taking care of her family. So this is what I always wanted to do. Be a wife and mother. But in reality, I cannot stay home and do those things because we can't support our family on one income alone. Because I am not able to stay at home, I get frustrated because my mind battles what I believed to be true in the past and what life is for me in the present.

Satan jumps in at these weak hours and tries to discourage me so that I will feel like I have failed. He makes me feel incomplete and that my life will never have any meaning because I never attained my childhood dreams. What a lie! Granted, my life may not have turned out the way I thought it would, but have I honestly considered that maybe it is better than I had planned?

Only God knows the bumps in the road ahead and perhaps, just perhaps, He steered me toward a safer and better course.

As women, we can get so wrapped up into the emotional feelings of failure, especially when they pertain to our careers. When we allow even one doubt to start pervading our minds, then Satan knows he's got us. You know that instant replay button we have in our minds when we relive a situation over and over again? It doesn't have to be that way! But we keep letting Satan push that button repeatedly and begin to live our lives wallowing in our own discouragement. I'm sick of it, aren't you? I don't want to live defeated and I know you don't want to live defeated. So we have to wise up to Satan's tricks!

But there's another side of this "work" coin. While some regret that they have to work, there are many that love it. Some love it so much that their priorities are constantly struggling to remain in balance. Please don't take this wrong. I am not saying that women should not work. Not at all! There are many women in the Bible who worked outside the home. Lydia sold fine fabrics, Deborah was one of the judges of Israel, and the list goes on. There is absolutely nothing wrong with enjoying your job. In fact, I wholeheartedly agree with the saying that goes, "Love what you do, and do what you love!" There is nothing better in life than loving what you are doing.

We have to be careful, though, when we enjoy the work that we're doing because Satan will try to get us distracted from the things should be most important in our lives. He can sugar coat any situation and make us crave more. He wants us to enjoy our work so much that we exclude the other priorities that need to be addressed in our lives.

This reminds me of my carbohydrate cravings. The more I feed my body carbohydrates, the more it seems to want. Pretty soon I am completely dependent on carbs and don't feel satisfied unless I give in to my cravings for them. Even if the rest of my body does not feel very good, I am trapped into believing if I just have a little more—a chewy brownie or a caramel candy—then I will feel better. When I wise up to my physical cravings and begin to put them in their proper places, then I can finally break myself from an overload of carbohydrates. At that point, I begin to eat because I'm hungry—not because I'm satisfying my cravings. Only then does my body start to feel normal again.

Satan knows this vicious cycle and is ready to trap us inside of it. He knows what makes us tick. Like carbohydrate addictions and others, he knows that kudos at work only serve to make us work harder so that we can be recognized. He knows the rush that success evokes and he keeps us striving for more and setting more goals, no matter the cost. He falsely convinces us that our success at work is more important than our personal relationship with God and our precious time with family. He is such a master deceiver! He is trying to make us ineffective for the kingdom by turning our attention to other things. We must watch out for his crafty ways!

But there's another area with work that sometimes gets overlooked. It's the area of temptation. For some, the temptation at work involves little things, like taking supplies or taking advantage of a trusting employer. But for others, the temptation is greater and goes beyond what many would consider minor offenses—it's the temptation of the flesh. We see people and things that we shouldn't be involved with, yet we give in to the pressure to become a part of the group. We struggle to balance the right from the wrong but get swayed in the wrong direction over and over again. Eventually we are hooked on these temptations, and if we behaved in any other fashion, then our coworkers would think there was something wrong with us. These actions that manifested themselves during our moments of temptation become customary behaviors at work and begin to define who we are in front of our coworkers.

Temptation is tough to battle. Our minds begin to conjure up thoughts that we shouldn't be thinking. What an inner struggle this is to those who know God's perfect plan yet choose to dabble in the areas of sin. Satan is thrilled when this happens because he has once again found an easy target. We must be on the constant lookout for his schemes or we will be drawn into his traps. We have to remember what the Bible says in 1 John 2:16, "*For everything in the world—the cravings of sinful man, the lust of his eyes and the boasting of what he has and does—comes not from the Father but from the world.*"

But work is not our only priority underneath God and our families. Our work should go hand in hand with our calling in life. Some people refer to this as ministry. Now I am aware that there are some lay people and some Bible scholars that would disagree with me on this point, but if you hear me out, I think I can explain.

There has always been a debate that work comes first and then ministry. But there has always been a counter debate against it that claims that it should be ministry first and then work because of the Great Commission. Since I am such an analytical person, I have mused over this argument many times. The conclusion that I have come to is that they are basically inseparable.

Look at it this way. My ministry should trickle into my work place because I am a living testimony of Jesus Christ wherever I am. Yet my work should trickle into my ministry because I cannot leave my calling at home for eight hours and then resume where I left off when I get home. I have been mandated to bring God's principles into every area of my life. While I am at work, I am to be a light to those around me who don't know Christ. How else will they see God if I don't do my part? This reminds me of the lyrics to an old song that goes like this: "We may be the only Jesus that some may ever see." We never know who may be watching, so our calling has to go with us to work each day.

For a new Christian, the thought of one's ministry or calling can be very alluring and fun. It can also be very rewarding. Because of the multitudes of ministry opportunities that are available in most churches, Christians have many choices to pick from. Sometimes we can find ourselves volunteering for too many things because of the "good feeling" that comes from serving the Lord. A word of caution would be to not get in too deep and too fast. It is important for Christians to be growing while they are serving, otherwise they will get burned out and become unfruitful which would become a stumbling block to others. We can never neglect personal growth and focus all our attention on ministry. We have to meet our priority to God first and then everything else we need will trickle downward in the order of our priorities.

Besides being involved in ministry at church among believers, we also have another ministry opportunity. Since most women have to work, the workplace naturally becomes our other mission field or "ministry." For those who can't go off to a foreign country and serve, we must embrace our "Jerusalem" and try to reach them with the Gospel. So how do we make this our ministry focus? We have to live each day believing that we are being watched and our actions are being judged by our coworkers. We must be constantly mindful that our guard must be up. Satan won't stop at anything to tear our witness down at work. The tiniest inconsistency at work will be pounced on and exploited. Knowing that he's out there just waiting to destroy our testimony should prompt us to keep fighting the good fight of faith. If we remain true to our walk with Christ, then we can make a difference. A little personal discomfort along the way doesn't compare to the payoff of changed lives in our workplace.

It's important to remember that as we focus on our ministry opportunities, Satan will be just around the corner waiting to stage a coupe. As we try to reach out and serve others, Satan wants us to reach in and serve self. He doesn't want others to see peace or happiness in our lives that comes from a personal relationship with our Savior. Oh no! He doesn't want you to try to make a difference in others lives. To him, our life witness is like a contagious disease that he has determined to turn into his mission to eradicate. Instead, he will try to continually change our focus to "self" and how we are feeling in an effort to keep us from spreading the redeeming and life-changing love of Jesus Christ. We must be on guard.

All of this talk of career and ministry reminds me of a lady in the Bible called Lydia. So let's travel back to the second missionary journey of Paul nearly two thousand years ago...

Lydia smoothed the threads of the cloth with her hands. "This particular tapestry was probably the prettiest one she had made this week," she thought. As she began to fold the stunning fabric, she noticed that its purple color seemed different than her others. It seemed to leap out and light up her tired eyes. The shade was so vibrant. Perhaps she had soaked it just a bit longer than usual? She'd have to remember to do that again. "Don't do the ordinary!" she made a mental note for next week. She would keep trying something different.

Her focus turned inward. "Usual. Her life was pretty ordinary and usual," she mused. She wasn't complaining, oh no! She was successful in every sense of the word. Her passion for purple and for weaving fine tapestries and silks had given her purpose. And it had made her extremely wealthy. Her father had been so proud of her success. He would gloat, "Who needs a man in your life if you're doing just fine on your own!" For years she had been tormented by his appeals to marry, but she couldn't bear to marry the men in her city. She didn't know why she felt so strongly, but she couldn't shake her general disappointment with the way they conducted themselves. Consequently, she never entertained the idea. Instead, she had consumed herself with her business and had made a considerable amount of money.

You could say that her life had changed the moment she had pursued her dream to make fine purple fabrics.

In general, she was happy with where she was in life except for one little thing. She wasn't quite sure what it was, but she was nearly convinced that it had something to do with this Jewish God that she had heard about. She had begun attending a small gathering by the river where they talked of this God. She felt in her heart that He was connected to this missing link in her life.

As a child she had worshipped the idols of Philippi. She was not Jewish and the land of Israel was far, far away. She searched for peace at her own city's temple but, instead, had found unrest. The questions about gods and life that she had stored in her heart never seemed to be answered there. But at the riverside gathering, she always felt differently. It seemed that this God was alive and that He cared about her. Each time that she went, more of her questioning thoughts began to make sense. Until she understood more, she would keep going there to worship Him. In fact, tomorrow was the Sabbath. As a maker of fine fabrics, she had better make sure she had something to wear.

When the Sabbath dawned, Lydia sprang out of bed and began dressing for the riverside gathering. She had a reputation to uphold. A seller of purple couldn't be seen in unsatisfactory attire. Why, no one would ever buy her cloth again! They would think that her personal clothing was a reflection of the quality of her goods. So she must proudly wear her finery. As she latched her sandals and placed glistening bracelets on her wrists, she started her trek toward the river. It wasn't too far away. It was just past the edge of town. The time of walking was perfect for practicing prayers for this Jewish God that she had begun to worship.

As she neared the river, she smiled at her female friends and acquaintances. They had been a great encouragement to her as she had started on this journey to find God. She was anxious to gather with them again and learn some more.

But what was this? There were men headed towards them. Were they here to break up the meeting? Why had they journeyed from town to join them at their gathering place?

The men were quick to reassure them that they were not there to disband their meeting. In fact, quite the opposite was true. They were there to speak to them! The leader of the group, Paul, began to talk in detail about the Jewish God. He spoke words that seemed to answer all her questions. It was if he knew what she was searching for. As he told them how Jesus had died on the cross for their sins, she opened her heart to the saving message. She knew without a doubt that this was what she had always been looking for. She had been searching for a Savior.

She was honored to take place in the baptism at the river. She was moved by its representation of the Savior's death, burial, and resurrection. How was it possible to know Someone for just a short time but feel that she had known Him forever? She didn't want to let go of this incredible peace she had in her heart.

As the men made motions to leave, she pleaded with them to come to her house and rest. "You have come so far, you must need to rest for awhile as you prepare for the work of the Lord."

Paul and his helper, Silas, agreed to her suggestion and began to use her house as a base camp for their ministry. They held prayer meetings with the believers of Philippi and shared their desire to see all of Macedonia come to know this Jesus that they preached. It had humbled and amazed Lydia to find out that she was the first convert in Macedonia! Up to this point, those accepting the salvation message had lived in Asia. Paul told her that God had told him through a dream at night that he needed to go to her people, and he obeyed. She was so glad he had come! His obedience to God had changed her life eternally.

Just knowing this new Jesus wasn't enough, though. She couldn't wait to tell her family and acquaintances at work about this Christ. He had cleansed her life from sin and Paul had said that they should share their stories with those around them. According to Jesus' last words, she could be a missionary right here in her hometown.

She was so thankful to play a small part in Paul's missionary journey. She knew that he would someday leave her city, but she was willing to keep this salvation message alive while he was gone. The change in her life had been real. The questions she had answered were real. Everything about this God was real and she was determined to let all who would listen know how He could change their lives.

What a story! Imagine what it must have been like to be there in person. It is such an encouragement to see a woman in the Bible who may have lived a life similar to ours. She worked and was quite successful at what she did. She balanced her work with her ministry. In the city of Philippi, she was the headquarters for Paul on his journeys. The letter to the Philippians was sent to the church that had most likely found its roots in Lydia's own home! Oh, to be used by God to that magnitude. But wait, yes, we can be used in the same way that Lydia was!

Let's think about Lydia's life for a moment. In Acts 16, we find out some more interesting facts about her. Look at verses 13 through 15. They say,

> *"On the Sabbath we (Paul and Silas) went outside the city gate to the river, where we expected to find a place of*

prayer. We sat down and began to speak to the women who had gathered there. One of those listening was a woman named Lydia, a dealer in purple cloth from the city of Thyatira, who was a worshiper of God. The Lord opened her heart to respond to Paul's message. When she and the members of her household were baptized, she invited us to her home. "If you consider me a believer in the Lord," she said, "Come and stay at my house." And she persuaded us."

And finally, in the last verse of this chapter, we read that after some time had passed, she was used by God again. Acts 16:40 says,

"After Paul and Silas came out of the prison, they went to Lydia's house, where they met with the brothers and encouraged them. Then they left."

What can we learn from Lydia's example in these verses? And how can we compare it to our own lives? Let's take a look:

- She worked. We work.

- She came to know the true Savior. We've come to know the true Savior.

- She extended her home and resources for the ministry. We can extend our own homes and resources for the ministry.

- She was faithful to the Lord. We can be counted faithful to the Lord.

- She was an example of God's love to her family. We can be an example of God's love to our families.

- She had fellowship with believers. We can fellowship with believers.

Lydia was able to do everything with a semblance of ease. She had an incredible testimony. She worked and was successful. She was able to minister while she was working, and not let things get out of control. She seemed to have her priorities right where God would want them. You may be thinking what I am thinking right now. "Who would not be able to get everything in order with Paul right there to guide you?" I admit that having Paul around to ask advice whenever she needed it was probably a very helpful thing for Lydia. But think of what we have been given to guide us that she didn't have. We have God's Holy Word in its entirety!

Because of this priceless possession, we cannot find any excuse that would keep us from living a life that mirrors Lydia's faithfulness. Knowing that we have the upper hand in the age that we live in where so many of the mysteries of the Bible have been revealed to us, leaves us without an excuse. Think about it. Our knowledge can become power! So let's tap into this power from on High and fight against the temptations of the devil that we struggle against so much. It's time to protect our outer circle of priorities in the areas of career and ministry.

Steps to Protect

Where do we even begin when we are trying to protect ourselves in the workplace and in ministry? There are so many angles that we can hone in on but I feel that it is best to be simple. When you are honest about where God has placed you in this world, then it will help you to come to peace with your life in this area of your priorities. God's Word has quite a bit to say about our influence in the world. In fact, more than you would think! So let's take a look at what the Bible says by using an acrostic pattern for the word "WORLD." The Bible always holds the answers to all our questionings and wonderings, so we can be assured that it will help us once again.

W - O - R - L - D

W – Wisdom

Wisdom is a great quality to attain. Many women will get a job just to learn more and feel more useful to society but God's view of wisdom has a slightly different meaning from that. He does not just view wisdom as a source of personal gain, but He also sees it as a means to more effectively serve Him and fulfill His plans for our lives. The Bible, especially in the book of Proverbs, is full of admonitions to gain wisdom. Take a look at what one passage has to say about wisdom. Proverbs 4:5-7 says,

"Get wisdom, get understanding; do not forget my words or swerve from them. Do not forsake wisdom, and she will protect you; love her, and she will watch over you. Wisdom is supreme; therefore get wisdom. Though it cost you all you have, get understanding."

There should be no doubt in our minds after reading these verses that God wants us to get wisdom. He told us to get it over and over again. Matthew Henry puts the meaning of this so eloquently. His commentary reads, "First, Get this wisdom, get this understanding…Pray for it, take pains for it, give diligence in the use of all appointed means to attain it. Wait at wisdom's gate…get possession of wise principles and the habits of wisdom. Get wisdom by experience, get it above thy getting, be more in care and take more pains to get this than to get the wealth of this world; whatever thou forgettest, get this; reckon it a great achievement, and pursue it accordingly."

Some think that God's wisdom is elusive, but in actuality, God can give us the wisdom we need if we will just ask for it and seek it. James 1:5 states,

"If any of you lacks wisdom, he should ask God, who gives generously to all without finding fault and it will be given to him."

Our wisdom does not have to come solely from the world through attending school and universities. We don't have to work to get the wisdom that this verse is talking about. Instead, a wisdom that is gained through an understanding of God is the best wisdom we could ever have. This kind of wisdom will direct you down all the avenues you want to go. With God's help and guidance, you'll be constantly headed in the right direction.

The Holman Illustrated Bible Dictionary gives a great definition for wisdom. It says,

> "Three basic definitions of wisdom summarize the status of the field of study very well. Note that the first two of these definitions are quite secular in nature while the third is religious. First, wisdom is considered by many to be simply the art of learning how to succeed in life… Second, wisdom is considered by some to be a philosophical study of the essence of life…Third, though the other definitions might include this, it seems that the real essence of wisdom is spiritual, for life is more than just living by a set of rules and being rewarded in some physical manner. Undoubtedly in this sense wisdom comes from God (Proverbs 2:6). Thus, though it will involve observation and instruction, it really begins with God and one's faith in Him as Lord and Savior."

When wisdom gives us divine direction, that is when we will discover that Satan wants to pull us off our course. We have to remember that Satan doesn't want us to influence the world around us, so he is setting up road blocks and booby traps to deter us. Since we know his tactics and what he is up to, we need to ignore his attempts to distract us and keep pressing onward. The more we know and have wisdom, the more we can accomplish for God.

The search for wisdom as women is one that began at the very beginning of time. In Genesis 3:6 we see that Eve desired this very thing! Here's what the Bible says in Genesis:

> "*When the woman saw that the fruit of the tree was good for food and pleasing to the eye, and also desirable for gaining wisdom, she took some and ate it. She also gave some to her husband, who was with her, and he ate it.*"

We all know the end of this story—it altered mankind's existence forever. But what else does the Bible say about wisdom? Here are some verses that will help us to gain godly wisdom as we reside in the world and try to reach the people around us.

Psalm 111:10 "*The fear of the LORD is the beginning of wisdom; all who follow his precepts have good understanding. To him belongs eternal praise.*"

Proverbs 17:24 "*A discerning man keeps wisdom in view, but a fool's eyes wander to the ends of the earth.*"

Luke 21:15 "*For I will give you words and wisdom that none of your adversaries will be able to resist or contradict.*"

James 1:5 "*If any of you lacks wisdom, he should ask God, who gives generously to all without finding fault, and it will be given to him.*"

James 3:17 "*But the wisdom that comes from heaven is first of all pure; then peace-loving, considerate, submissive, full of mercy and good fruit, impartial and sincere.*"

So what can we learn from these verses? Here are five simple lessons about wisdom that we need to take to heart:

1. To get wisdom, we have to ask for it. James 1:5 tells us that if we lack wisdom, all we need to do is ask God for it. (Also see Ephesians 1:17 and Colossians 1:9)

2. To have wisdom, we must fear God. If we want to have a deeper understanding of the world around us, we must respect and fear our Heavenly Father. This is the true beginning of wisdom according to Psalm 111:10.

3. If we want to be successful, then we must keep God's wisdom in view according to Proverbs 17:24.

4. If we want to defend our faith, then Luke 21:15 says that we can use the words and wisdom that we have been given.

5. If we want to know what kind of wisdom we've been given, then we can look at James 3:17 where it says that it's pure, peace-loving, considerate, submissive, full of mercy and good fruit, impartial and sincere.

God wants our Christian walk to be a positive experience. He wants us to enjoy the blessings of obedience that comes from a life that is fully committed to Him. That is why He put over 200 references to wisdom in the Bible. He knew that we would need to protect our minds and hearts in this worldly battle against Satan, so he gave us the formula for wisdom that will help us.

O – Obligation

While we are living in this world, we find that we have many obligations. Work is no exception to this truth. Work is an obligation. It is an obligation of your life, your time, your decisions, and your resources. Now this obligation comes with another obligation if we look at Romans 4:4. It says, *Now when a man works, his wages are not credited to him as a gift, but as an obligation."*

The passage before verse 4 is discussing how Abraham could not have been justified by works because then he would have been able to boast in what he had done. Any benefit would have been obligated to him. So it is for us, whenever we work, we are owed an obligation from the person we worked for.

Unfortunately, we don't work just because we love or enjoy working. We work because there is some sort of benefit in it for us or for our families. We need the money to pay bills or to send our children to college. So, according to this verse and societies conventions, our workplace has an obligation to pay us for our labor, but we are also obligated to them in order for us to receive those wages. Our life is not entirely our own when we make a commitment to work. We are obligated to our workplace.

But we are also obligated by Christ to share the Gospel while we are living in this world. The Great Commission tells us that we must go into all of the world and preach the Gospel to every person. We have a spiritual duty to fulfill as well. We cannot ignore the calling that God has placed on every Christian's life. We MUST go and we MUST tell. To be in obedience to Christ, we have to follow His explicit commands.

Our obligations piggy back on the wisdom that we need to protect ourselves from Satan's grasp. If we have the wisdom from above that God is freely willing to give us, then our obligations are fulfilled through the power of Christ. Without this heavenly wisdom front and center in our lives, we become powerless to fulfill our mission. We must have both working in unison to complete our earthly purpose.

R – Responsibility

Responsibility is almost the same as obligation but has a slightly different bend to it. Responsibility becomes personal. Responsibility knows that unless we follow God's steps that are laid out for us, everything we do is in vain.

Jesus, through the words of John 4:35, tells us, *"Do you not say, 'Four months more and then the harvest'? I tell you, open your eyes and look at the fields! They are ripe for harvest."* Jesus is stressing the urgency of our calling. He is telling us that the time is NOW. The harvest of souls is ready for us and we cannot delay anymore. However, isn't it easy to make excuses for our lack of action? We console ourselves into thinking that we can put off our God-given duties until tomorrow. But how many times have we found that tomorrow is too late? Even Christ told us in Matthew 6:34 that we are not to worry about tomorrow. It says, *"Therefore do not worry about tomorrow, for tomorrow will worry about itself. Each day has enough trouble of its own."*

But our responsibility is laid out even clearer in 1 Peter 2:12. It encourages us to: *"Live such good lives among the pagans that, though they accuse you of doing wrong, they may see your **good** deeds and glorify God on the day he visits us."*

It is our responsibility to live good lives! Once we have tasted the goodness of the Lord, there should be no turning back.

This reminds me of the old song entitled "I Have Decided to Follow Jesus." The words of the song say: "I have decided to follow Jesus, I have decided to follow Jesus, I have decided to follow Jesus, no turning back, no turning back." When we decide to lay our past aside and look toward the promise of a future with Christ, we must not get sidetracked. We can't turn back. We must *"finish the race"* as Paul says in 2 Timothy 4:7. The world must see our good deeds. We have to be different in their eyes—not weird, but different. We must exhibit a difference that is appealing to those who are searching and alluring to those who are dissatisfied. Our lives should make others crave the things of God that they are missing.

L – Let Us Run with Perseverance

When we finally realize that we need wisdom, that we have

an obligation, and that we have a moral responsibility to those around us, we need to become willing to lay aside the things in our lives that keep us from doing what we should. Hebrews 12:1 says, *"Therefore, since we are surrounded by such a great cloud of witnesses, let us throw off everything that hinders and the sin that so easily entangles, and let us run with perseverance the race marked out for us."*

Once we finally get on the right track, we have to be faithful. How many Christians do you know who have fallen away? How many have stopped persevering? Too many, right? They failed to prepare their heart for the battle that Satan would wage against them. They did not prepare for the long haul. In order for us to survive, we have to gird up and bunker down with God's power and strength. Only then will we persevere through Satan's attacks.

D – Dig Deep into the Word

The last point in our acrostic for WORLD is the area of digging deeper into the Word of God. If we do not commit ourselves to personal Bible study and prayer, then we will never reach the potential God has for us. God gives us the perfect plan to reach our potential. He says in 2 Timothy 2:15 to *"Do your best to present yourself to God as one approved, a workman who does not need to be ashamed and who correctly handles the word of truth."*

If we follow His plan, we are assured of success. We will never be ashamed! We will correctly handle the Word of God as we share it with those around us.

I know digging deep can be a chore. I have been there! I have struggled with it. I have failed miserably in many areas. Until we realize that we can't function without God's Word, we will constantly stumble. Remember, Proverbs 14:1 says this,

"The wise woman builds her house, but with her own hands the foolish one tears hers down."

If we are truly wise with the wisdom that comes from God, then we will be able to protect our lives from the coming attacks of Satan by being constantly in the Word. When we start to get discouraged with Bible study, we need to remember our priorities—who we are serving and why He deserves our full devotion.

God does not want us to give up in the middle of serving Him. He placed us in this world so that we could bring honor and glory to Him. He wants our Christian walk to be a journey with an eternal destination, not just a walk around the block every now and then. We need to be focused on the task ahead of us. Just like Paul said that he had fought the good fight, finished the race, and kept the faith; we need to do the same.

I tell my son, Ryan, about this all the time. I remind him as he is struggling with college or wrestling with decisions, that he needs to keep his eyes on the goal. He can not get bogged down with all of the distractions that come his way. He must keep looking further down the road at the goal. That is the only way that he can get a glimpse of the prize.

We need to commit to serving God for a lifetime. Jesus set a great example for us. In John 5:17 it tells us,

"Jesus said to them, "My Father is always at his work to this very day, and I, too, am working."

Jesus didn't give up either! Since the beginning of the world, His plan was to redeem mankind. We are part of His eternal passion. So, in the spirit of John 5:17, we need to always be at our work, too. Don't get sidetracked along this journey called "life." This outer circle of work and ministry priorities that we are surrounded with can be the most rewarding yet.

Chapter 9

PROTECTING MY MIND FROM THE PAST

"Forget the former things; do not dwell on the past"
(Isaiah 43:18).

You may have heard the phrase "The past is passed!" It is a simple statement, yet the point of it rings clear. The past things in our lives are over with. There is no retrieving them. There is no reliving them. There is no redoing them. There is nothing that we can do about the past because it has passed in time.

Notice how that little phrase "The past is passed" mirrors the key verse from this chapter. Our verse in Isaiah 43:18 says, *"Forget the former things; do not dwell on the past."* Even God in His infinite wisdom knew that mankind would wrestle with their past. He knew that man had a sin nature and that he would inevitably sin because the only perfect human being would be Jesus Christ when He lived here on this earth. God knew that our sins would be remembered by us and would potentially become a noose around our necks. That noose would prevent us from living the Christian life that God had planned for us, so He lovingly addressed the issue for our benefit.

This feeling of condemnation that many women feel over

their past is similar to what the nation of Israel was feeling when Isaiah penned these words. Isaiah was discussing the deliverance of Israel in this passage and he was trying to encourage them to look ahead and not dwell on what had already transpired in their history. MacArthur makes this brief statement in reference to their deliverance, "Deliverances of the nation in the past will pale in comparison with the future deliverance the Lord will give His people." God wanted Israel to change their focus from backward to forward. He wanted them to look toward the salvation of the Lord instead of wallowing in the memories of the past. He knew that they would never make progress if they were constantly reflecting on the failures of yesteryear.

This reminds me of the story of the fork. You have probably heard it but it is worthy of repetition. An elderly lady made a simple request as she lay on her deathbed. She wanted to be buried with a fork. When asked "Why?" by her friends and family, she simply replied that life was a lot like dinner. You eat the main courses and sides while you are here on earth, but the best part—the dessert—comes at the very end. She wanted a fork in her hand so she could enjoy the sweet delicacies of heaven. Because according to her, "The best was yet to come!" What a beautiful realization that nothing in the past and nothing in the present could compare to a future in heaven!

As we look back to our verse, we see that it is full of redeeming peace for those who have struggled with sins of their past. Much like the fork, it gives hope for the future because we have been commanded not to "dwell on the past." I loved some of the comments that Matthew Henry made about this verse and the surrounding passage. Here are some of his interpretations. "For the encouragement of our faith and hope, it is good for us often to remember what God has done for his people against his and their enemies...He promises to do yet greater thing for them than he had done in the days of old..." Matthew Henry explains that by remembering all the events from the past they "...undervalue the present things" and forget that God is going to do more incredible things for them in the future. If we are constantly looking back at our past mistakes, will we never see the goodness and glory that God has prepared for us? Absolutely not! We don't want to "undervalue" the present that we are living in and the future that is to come. So we must, we MUST turn our focus forward.

I think that we would all agree that any sins that we committed in the past or in the present are grievous sins in the eyes of the Lord. Lying, envy, slander, gossip, anger, dependencies, abuse, and sexual temptations are just a few of the sins that we struggle with. These sins can be damaging and can ruin our lives by their consequences. But for most people, the most difficult sins to let go of and forgive themselves for are the sins that deal with sexual temptations. Counselors tell us that sexual sins result in the most damage to a person's emotional state of being because they are done "against" the body instead of "outside" of the body as other sins are. God's Word corroborates this in 1 Corinthians 6:18 where it explains:

> "*Flee sexual immorality. Every sin that a man does is outside the body, but he who commits sexual immorality sins against his own body*" (NKJV).

This is why there is such a battle in the soul when sexual sins have been committed. Satan knows this verse and what it means, so he is particularly pleased when we stumble into the areas of sexual impurities. Lust, pornography, flirtations, and pleasures that are to be experienced only within the confines of marriage are just a few of his tactics against us. He knows mankind's weaknesses in these areas so he strategizes and devises the perfect method of temptation that will cause us to fall. We have to be immersed in the Word to protect ourselves from these attacks because Christ is the only One who can deliver us.

Take a look at the following scenarios. As you read, notice how easily Satan can get a foothold into our lives and influence us to commit any type of sin. In a brief moment of time, he can destroy what we have taken years to build and to protect.

Marina shut the door gently behind her, hands trembling. Why was she being so careful to be quiet? No one would hear her anyway or even think that anything was amiss. But it was guilt—heavy, stabbing, suffocating guilt. She couldn't run. It was right there pounding through her core straight to her heart.

It was over. It was part of her past now. There was nothing she could do to erase it. It had really happened—to her, no less—by her own choice. It was her identity now—"I'm an adulteress," she breathed.

Just a few moments ago she had felt cherished and special. It was okay to feel that way, wasn't it? But her heart condemned her as she put her keys away.

Deep in her heart she knew the real truth. It wasn't supposed to happen that way. In fact, it wasn't supposed to happen at ALL. That private moment was only supposed to happen with her husband. She had taken a vow when they got married. WHAT had she done? WHY did she do it?

Her heart rebuked her as she put her keys away. But she took a deep breath and told herself, "If I'm not going to end this, then I'm just going to pretend it's no big deal. I'll act like it never happened. I'll just forget about it while I'm here at home." But as her conscience continued to condemn her, she added, "Better yet! I'll never see him again. Never! I'll never do anything like this again." Somehow, even after this declaration, she didn't feel any better.

Jessie put her hand back into her pocket. Why was she always using her hands to destroy instead of show love?

She had no excuse, not even her father's rampages when she was a child could justify what she was doing to her own children. She knew better. She had been the victim before. Her whole life seemed to be crumbling around her. Nothing ever seemed to go right. She was a failure at work. A failure at home. A failure with her friends. Was she stuck in this hopeless existence? Could her life ever be anything different? She desperately wanted it to be, but didn't know where to turn to for help. Her past would always haunt her...

———

Sadly, these stories sound very familiar. We have seen this despair in others and, perhaps, have even felt it in our own personal lives. We aren't alone in this personal vendetta against ourselves. Coworkers, friends, and even church members are dealing with this utter condemnation of body and soul. At times, we have even watched movies and read books that have dramatically played out these events. It didn't matter whether the characters were Christian or not. Our hearts have been torn out and twisted by stories like these. We can identify with and sense this deep devastation that these women feel, and our hearts break for them and sympathy pours out.

But it is possible that some women may not feel this type of sorrow when they have committed sins such as these. They go to the opposite extreme in these cases. Since these situations surround us so much in the media, I want to go so far as to suggest that we have become desensitized to the reproach that these sins are to God. Our sexual morality or our ability to control our actions just doesn't matter so much anymore. In fact, we can even overlook these sins just a wee little bit—because let's face it, "nobody is perfect" and "everyone makes mistakes."

Please don't tune me out right here. This is not going to be a Sunday sermon. I am simply stating the facts according to an

Almighty God's point of view. Did you know that this Almighty, all powerful God has provided freedom from all sin and especially from the ones that we have just mentioned? There are some incredible verses that He placed in His Word that can completely remove the condemnation we can feel from the sins of the past.

So many women know someone who has been through a valley like this in their lives. And many have even walked through it themselves. The shame and failure that godly women feel when they make mistakes that seem almost unforgivable is extremely overwhelming. And because these haunting sins in our past are usually devastating, personal sins, these broken women feel as if they can never be forgiven for them.

Oh, what a deceptive lie that is. Satan pounces on us immediately, like an animal on its prey, when we start to think this way. We can easily forgive others for sins like these—just not ourselves. WE aren't good enough to be forgiven. We think that our sins are a tiny bit worse than those around us and have reached the level of "unforgivable." We privately conclude that we are not good enough for forgiveness because of the types or quantities of sins we have committed. We feel that there is only enough grace for those around us and it could never extend to us. We are willing to hand out that grace in shovelfuls to others, but we are not worthy of even the littlest speck of grace or forgiveness for ourselves.

These are the lies Satan thrills to tell. He wants us to believe that we will never amount to anything. He exults, "Another sinner has fallen and thinks she can't get up!" But God is not honored when we think this way. As we begin to believe Satan's lies, God is calling us to forgiveness and continued service. But we are usually too busy to stop and listen. "Please don't bother me right now with this, God," we say in our minds, "I'm choosing worthlessness, despair, and humiliation as my penitence for this sin. It's a horrible sin that I just committed, so I may have to stay here in this hole of despondency for a good, long while." And Satan silently cheers us along. He has our mind in his grips now and he intends for it to stay there. Any attempt at freedom and forgiveness will be trampled immediately. There's no room for forgiveness in his world. "This is a good one!" he thinks. He's captured us and he's going to try to keep us in his trap (and actually without too much effort on his part) for as long as possible. "Yippee! Another pushover…" he gloats.

I don't know about you but I am just about sick of Satan's self-glorifying ways. He is not in charge here—we are! And through the power of Jesus Christ, we can claim the strength we need to persevere and proceed without a glance back at our failures. Dependencies are enslaving. Sexual sins are heinous. Abusive sins are despicable. Divisive sins are a disgrace to our character. There is absolutely no doubt about any of that. But no matter how far we have fallen into sin, our gracious God can pick us up from the depths where we have ended up.

Are we forgetting that He is the omnipresent God of this universe? There is no where for us to run that He cannot find us and rescue us. Your sins, and mine, are completely forgivable. The whitest lies and the blackest sins are entirely forgivable by a loving heavenly Father. We have to remember and claim the freeing truth in Mark 10:27 that says, "*Jesus looked at them and said, 'With man this is impossible, but not with God; all things are possible with God.'*" We can see from this verse that forgiveness from our past is completely possible with God.

So as you ponder these possibilities with God, why don't you sit back and relax for a moment and let me prove that all things are possible through a story in the Old Testament. But before we tell the story, let's go back in time to approximately 600 B.C. and set the stage.

The nation of Israel was divided into two parts at this time in history. After the reign of Solomon, the nation of Israel was split into a northern kingdom and a southern kingdom. The northern kingdom was made up of ten tribes and was called Israel. It had its own king to rule over them. The southern kingdom, called

Judah, was made up of two other tribes—Benjamin and Judah. Because Judah occupied most of the land in the southernmost area, the southern kingdom carried his name. Judah also had its own king that ruled over them. In fact, King David and the Lord Jesus Himself came from the tribe of Judah. (You may recall the verses that mention that Jesus is from the tribe of Judah. They are found in Psalm 78:68, Hebrews 7:14, and Revelation 5:5.) Jeremiah is now on the scene and has been commissioned by God to warn His people. This story from yesterday sounds a lot like today…

It was near the turn of the century of 600 B.C. Jeremiah, the weeping prophet, could not stop crying. He had a heavy heart for the children of Judah. They had turned away from the one true God and were worshipping the gods of the neighboring land. He had begged and pleaded with them. He had explained at length the judgment that was coming if they did not turn from their sins. But it was all to no avail. Their depravity of body and mind had minimized the position of a prophet of the Lord. Prophets were ridiculed now. No one seemed to care about the messages God was sending through the mouths of His chosen men.

Instead, the people continued happily in their sins. They had stripped the Temple of all its holy articles and had set up "high places, sacred stones, and wooden Asherah poles on every high hill and under every spreading tree" (I Kings 14:23). Because they had turned their backs on God and chosen idols instead, the Lord had called them adulterers. During the reign of King Josiah, the Lord had spoken His true feelings to Jeremiah and said, "Have you seen what faithless Israel has done? She has gone up on every high hill and under every spreading tree and has committed adultery there. I thought that after she had done all this she would return to me but she did not, and her unfaithful sister Judah saw it. I gave faithless Israel her certificate of divorce and sent her away because of all her adulteries. Yet I saw that her unfaithful sister Judah had no fear; she also went out and committed adultery. Because Israel's immorality mattered so little to her, she defiled the land and committed adultery with stone and wood" (Jeremiah 3:6-9).

As Jeremiah told them God's words, he was mocked again. How could this be? Couldn't they see the seriousness of their sins? Did they even acknowledge their actions as sin at all? He doubted it. What was wrong was now considered right in their eyes, and what had been right was now wrong! Jeremiah began to weep again.

God's messages made perfect sense to him. How could he convey to his brothers in Israel and Judah that they must repent? Why had he been chosen for this hopeless job? Surely there were other more qualified men that could have communicated better and would have received more respect than he had.

Despite his insecurities, God continued to speak to him about Israel and Judah's sinful adultery against Him. He said, "Why should I forgive you? Your children have forsaken me and sworn by gods that are not gods. I supplied all their needs, yet they committed adultery and thronged to the houses of prostitutes." And then He went on to say, "Will you steal and murder, commit adultery and perjury, burn incense to Baal and follow other gods you have not known?" God took their sin of idolatry seriously. He took it personally. To Him, their idol worship was a direct reflection of their hearts. They had turned their hearts from Him and given them to another—just as if they had sexually given their bodies to them. God viewed their devotion to Him as sacred. Just as a husband is toward his wife, He desired that they would view Him as their One and Only, never to be separated from His love.

"Why couldn't they see this?" Jeremiah bemoaned. The first book of Moses had said, "For this reason a man will leave his father and mother and be united to his wife, and they will become one flesh." One flesh…that was never to be torn apart. Israel and Judah had torn themselves away from God and they didn't even seem to care!

Jeremiah plodded on—dejected. Yet he continued to proclaim God's message of doom and disaster over and over again to them, his heart breaking within him as he pleaded for their repentance from these adulterous acts. They had to know what they were doing was wrong. It was evil in God's sight.

"Jerusalem will fall," he cried out, "Turn from your wicked sins or Jerusalem will fall!"

But his pleas and cries fell on deaf ears. In spite of all the warnings, the children of Judah did not want to believe that these terrible things would actually happen to them. Instead, they listened to false prophets and diviners who told them the things that they wanted to hear. "Peace, peace! You will be just fine!" the false prophets and diviners said. "Don't worry about your possessions, cities, and land. Nothing will happen to them. You will be all right."

So the children of Judah refused to listen to Jeremiah and chose to believe the diviners' lies. It was easier to believe their lies than take action to repent. (Sound familiar?) They were quite comfortable with the way things were. Why change anything if you didn't really have to? So they settled back and continued to live in their daily sins with no more thought of the judgment that Jeremiah preached. Nothing would happen to them. Everything would be just fine…

Jeremiah, dejected and defeated, took his rest for

the night. His tears came again as he laid his weary body down. He would sleep and then get up again tomorrow and do the exact same thing that he did today. The message never changed. However hopeless it seemed, he would continue to proclaim the warnings of his holy God until his dying breath.

I almost have to take a deep breath after that story. How could they not have seen the warning signs all around them? Couldn't they see the passion of Jeremiah's heart? How could they have dismissed his pleas without a second thought? I just don't understand! I am floored that after all that Israel and Judah had been through, and the miracles and blessings that were poured out on them by Jehovah God, that they would even act like this.

If God's words were always true before, why would it be any different now? Come on! Really? Would they be exempt this time? I don't think so! I guess I must concede that they were probably just like everyone else around them—trying to live their lives as good as "they" knew how and forgetting that God is ultimately in control and knows best. Hindsight is 20/20, right? I'm sure they kicked themselves over and over after all of Jeremiah's warnings came true.

The Bible tells us in 2 Kings 24:6-12, 2 Chronicles 36:8-10, and Daniel 1:1-2 of the very fall of Judah that Jeremiah had prophesied. Judah's King Jehoiachin (son of King Jehoiakim), who at the time was 18 years old and had only reigned for three months, was handed over to King Nebuchadnezzar of Babylon and taken into exile. He wasn't the only one captured though. There were children of Judah, officials, craftsmen, and artisans that were captured and carried into exile, too. All this took place around 597 B.C. Yet even after this mass exodus into exile, Jeremiah continued to prophesy about this time of captivity for the children of Judah.

Jeremiah 29:10 explains the extent of their punishment. He

wanted them to be prepared for what would happen to them. It states, "This is what the Lord says, 'When seventy years are completed for Babylon, I will come to you and fulfill my gracious promise to bring you back to this place.'" The children of Judah finally repented and cried out to the Lord during this time of captivity. They were fearful and terrified (Jeremiah 30:4) and God in his loving mercy heard them and began to comfort them.

When they realized that they were in Babylon for the long haul—seventy years, I know their hearts must have collapsed within them. It is hard to be strong for such a long time. An hour, a day—we can handle that. But weeks, months, and even years, that is hard! Many of the captives grieved that they would never be able to go back. They were thirty, forty, fifty years old, and even older. They would die in Babylon. They would never see their homeland again. How sad that would be. Sometimes our own sinful consequences can be more than we can bear. The outcome of what the Lord had said, while devastatingly final for some, gave promise and hope to others. This exile *would* come to an end. They would someday be able to go back home.

Can you imagine what the children of Judah were going through? The minute they were ushered out of their houses they had to have instantly realized that they had been wrong. They made a BIG mistake. They shouldn't have worshipped other gods and removed the sacred articles from the Temple. They should have listened to Jeremiah! If they had really listened to what he had said, they would have repented. He was the Lord's prophet after all. He had a direct connection to Jehovah. Even so, what was done—was done.

This reminds me of when we choose to sin...we sinned, we did it, and there's no taking it back. Now what are we going to do about it? How are we going to fix things? The consequences of our sin loom just around the corner. We can't run from it.

Despite the fact that the children of Judah had to suffer the consequences of their immoral sins, God in His loving way tries to comfort them during this scary and uncertain time. Imagine how lonely and deserted they felt. They had lost everything. ... Just as our reputation can be lost when we make poor choices at work and home. ...Just as our influence can be lost when we succumb to the temptations of the world. ...Just as our purity can be lost when we freely give ourselves to someone other than our intended spouse.

But in spite of all the children of Judah's sinful doings, God continues with His message of comfort to them in Jeremiah 29:11. Here we see the familiar and often quoted verse :

> " 'For I know the plans I have for you,' declares the Lord, 'plans to prosper you and not to harm you, plans to give you hope and a future.' "

The consequences of their sins were bleak, but their future was bright according to the Lord. They had a hope that they could cling to. In spite of everything, we see in this 29th chapter of Jeremiah, that God's hands are full of tenderness and mercy as He reaches down to them.

As we ponder their dilemma, we have to believe somewhere in our minds that the children of Judah finally "got it." All that Jeremiah warned them about had come to pass. One hundred percent of what he had said came true. I am sure that now when he said something they were listening very, very closely. Like anybody, when you are in a desperate situation, even the slightest glimmer of hope is held onto tightly.

So, since they were in exile for a while, now what? There was not much that they could do. They had to wait out their punishment just like the children of Israel hundreds of years before had to wander aimlessly around in the desert for forty years until God would allow them to enter the Promised Land.

As the seventy years of exile drew to a close, we see the children of Judah once again. They were different than before. They knew they had blown it. They had borne the consequences of their sins as they were in captivity. It is at this point that we see the Lord's encouraging, prophetic words which remind His children once again of their eventual release. He spoke to them gently and reassuringly in the following passages. Take a look at what He said in Jeremiah 31:16-22a.

> [16] *"This is what the LORD says: 'Restrain your voice from weeping and your eyes from tears, for your work will be rewarded,' declares the LORD. 'They will return from the land of the enemy.* [17] *So there is hope for your future,' declares the LORD. 'Your children will return to their own land.'*
>
> [18] *'I have surely heard Ephraim's moaning: "You disciplined me like an unruly calf, and I have been disciplined. Restore me, and I will return, because you are the LORD my God.* [19] *After I strayed, I repented; after I came to understand, I beat my breast. I was ashamed and humiliated because I bore the disgrace of my youth."*
>
> [20] *'Is not Ephraim my dear son, the child in whom I delight? Though I often speak against him, I still remember him. Therefore my heart yearns for him; I have great compassion for him,' declares the LORD.*
>
> [21] *'Set up road signs; put up guideposts. Take note of the highway, the road that you take. Return, O Virgin Israel, return to your towns.* [22] *How long will you wander, O unfaithful daughter?"*

In this passage, we see that God yearned for them (v.20). He told them there was hope for their future (v.17) He had great compassion for them (v.20) In spite of all they had done, He loved them with an incredible love—a love so deep that He *yearned* for them. Does this sound like a God who doesn't care about us? Is this a God who expels us from His incomprehensible love and mercy? Not at all. This is a God who loves incredibly and forgives sufficiently. His abundant grace is available to anyone who believes it.

Now take a moment and read verse 21 again in our passage. I had to point this out, especially for women. Look at it closely. In fact, read it again and again until you really hear what it has to say. "…Return, O Virgin Israel…" It really says it. Virgin. Once they had been considered adulterers and adulteresses, now He was calling them virgins. The adulterous Israel, which included Judah, is being asked to return. But this time it's not as an adulteress, it's as a virgin. Yes! You read right! Oh, the incredible power of the Lord God's forgiveness. It is too hard to be fathomed, but it is desperately sought by the wounded and sinful soul. Like adulterous Judah and Israel, those who have succumbed to sins that now haunt them, feel the finality and condemnation of their burden. And it is only a righteous God, our God, who can make things right.

Did you know that the word virgin in this verse specifically refers to a "virgin"? I know some will be doubtful, but it is right there in black and white. I even looked it up in Hebrew. The word virgin is not just a symbolic reference here—it is the same word used throughout the Bible when it talks specifically about a virgin woman. It is even the same word used to describe Isaac's wife-to-be, Rebekah, in Genesis 24:16a.

> *"The girl was very beautiful, a virgin; no man had ever lain with her."*

We also can see from the context of this passage that Israel's and Judah's whole issue was that of adultery. So as restoration was granted, why would "virgin" mean anything else? That would not match the context. I had to read this passage in Jeremiah over and over as it sank in. God didn't see them as adulterers anymore, they were virgins. Fully restored to Him.

As mentioned previously, counselors say that sexual sins are some of the most devastating sins for women to deal with. Without proper counseling, a contrite heart, and forgiveness from God, their lives seem to flounder in despair. It is hard for them to realize that God is still willing to use them to further His purpose. Instead, they feel abandoned and unworthy of the forgiveness of a Savior. If Christ has offered us full restoration, then why do some believers reject His complete forgiveness? Why can't we accept His mercy and grace when we do things that seem unforgivable? Why? Because Satan doesn't want us to accept this forgiveness!

We have to remember that when God forgives us, it is complete, it is over, it is in the past. And based on God's Word, we are not to dwell on it. The problem is that we don't understand what "justification" means. The *Holman Illustrated Bible Dictionary* defines it this way, it is the "Divine, forensic act of God, based on the work of Christ upon the cross, whereby a sinner is pronounced righteous by the imputation of the righteousness of Christ." The best way that I have heard it explained is like this—it simply means "just as if I never sinned." That is how God sees us when we ask for cleansing and forgiveness. No matter what sins we have committed that have put us into our own "exile," God still regards us as worthy and good. Jeremiah 24:5b says, "...I regard as good the exiles from Judah, whom I sent away from this place to the land of the Babylonians."

His eyes see us as righteous and holy before Him once again. Our sin does not matter to Him anymore. It has been forgiven. It has been covered by the blood of Jesus Christ.

The problem that most of us have with forgiveness comes from our inner self. It is our own minds that sabotage our efforts at reconciliation. Consequently, we keep digging and digging at a pit we feel that we belong in—a Slough of Despond like we see in the book *Pilgrim's Progress*. Do we truly know that His mercy and forgiveness set us free from this trap? Believe this truth, cling to this truth, claim this truth, and continue to live victoriously in this truth! You are completely cleansed if you just simply ask Him to forgive you. It really is that easy. If past sins have defeated you today, don't wait any longer. Claim that freeing power that God graciously grants to all who genuinely repent. Why don't we ask for forgiveness right now?

But beware...even as we are praying, Satan will try to convince us that we are not worthy of forgiveness and that we don't deserve restoration. Don't listen to his deceit. God is ready to grant complete forgiveness. If He can take the sinful, disgusting, and adulterous Israel back into His arms and see them as virgins once again, He can do the same for us. As we recognize that we have hope for forgiveness from our personal penitentiary of past mistakes, we need to protect ourselves from falling into Satan's subtle traps. Let's take a look at some steps to protect ourselves in the area of past mistakes.

Steps to Protect

As we make this personal application, I want you to be encouraged that we can all move forward with hope in our hearts, no matter what our past sins have been. Everyone can finish this chapter with renewed hope, renewed fire, and a renewed promise of freedom to share with others. Remember, we do not live under the law any more, we live under grace. And that grace grants us freedom through the shed blood of Jesus Christ. His blood covers it all—from the best to the worst in us—it is all covered by His mercy and grace. That is why we can take these rich passages from Jeremiah and make a personal application today to our own lives. The very same hope that Jeremiah preached of in days of old can be held onto today if you will just believe in and claim God's power in your life.

Let's look back now at Jeremiah 24:5-8. God very clearly gave the children of Judah a promise of hope which included six steps that they needed to accept and understand during their time of exile. Like the children of Judah, we can claim these promises in our own lives too, when we have been defeated by sinful failures. Examine what each of these verses is trying to tell us.

"I regard as good the exiles from Judah." v. 5

The first step toward hope is realizing that we are worthy of God's salvation. We need to remember that no matter what has happened to us or what we have done, if we have accepted Christ as our personal Lord and Savior, then we are His children. He regards us as "good." He loves us with an unending love and never wants to lose us to anything or anybody else. In true humility, we have to come to Him. When we do this, He lovingly accepts and receives us back to Himself. Just as a mother can never remove her thoughts of her children once they are born, our heavenly Father will not forget about us. Why? Because our children *belong* to us! Our lives are centered around their well-being and they are worthy of our love.

"My eyes will watch over them for their good." v. 6

The second step toward hope is understanding that God is watching over us.

Psalm 34:15 states, *"The eyes of the Lord are on the righteous and His ears are open to their cry."* Let's make a personal connection to this. Think about this example: We pay people in childcare to watch our children. This "watching" that they provide and we pay for shows that we care about our children. Someone is there with them and it gives us peace of mind.

Just like this example, we can know that we are not alone in this battle. God is with us every step of the way. He is watching our every move. He is there. He will be faithful to complete every good work in us. Hebrews 13:20, 21 says,

> *"Now may the God of peace who brought up our Lord Jesus from the dead, that great Shepherd of the sheep, through the blood of the everlasting covenant,* ***make you complete in every good work to do His will, working in you what is well pleasing in His sight****, through Jesus Christ, to whom be glory forever and ever. Amen"* (NKJV).

He constantly has us in His sight—in plain view—as He desires and works with us to do His will.

"I will bring them back to this land." v. 6

The third step toward hope is that God will bring us back from this place we find ourselves in. Wherever our sin or circumstances have taken us, we don't have to remain there forever! We have to make a choice. We can remain just as we are for the rest of our lives, or we can decide to make a difference in our future. We can repent. We can determine to change our actions or outcomes. With God's help, WE CAN do this. We will be looking at three steps in just a minute that will help us know how to come back to God. But for now, remember this—He will bring us BACK if we just let Him!

"I will build them up and not tear them down." v. 6

The fourth step toward hope is to know that God's plan is to build us up! So many times we take the negative approach here and say to ourselves. "What is God doing? This can't be right! This is terrible. It doesn't make sense. Why is this happening to me? It isn't fair!" God's ultimate goal for you and I is to realize that He is working everything for our good (Romans 8:28). Even the bad things that happen in our lives can be used for God's glory.

This reminds me of the illustration of the Potter in Jeremiah 18:3-6. It says,

> *"So I went down to the potter's house, and I saw him working at the wheel. But the pot he was shaping from the clay was marred in his hands; so the potter formed it into another pot, shaping it as seemed best to him. Then the word of the Lord came to me 'O house of Israel, can I not do with you as this potter does?' declares the Lord. 'Like clay in the hand of the potter, so are you in my hand, O house of Israel'."*

God will completely take us and build in us an incredible Christian testimony if we will let Him. He will mold and shape our lives if we will allow Him free access to cleanse every corner of our hearts. He has great plans for us. He came down to this earth and commissioned us to be witnesses and spread His story to the world. He does not want us to remain useless while we are here. He is ready to build us into effective witnesses for Him. That has been His plan all along.

"I will plant them and not uproot them." v. 6

The fifth step towards hope is realizing that God wants to give us stability. Of this one thing I am sure. God is in control. He doesn't want us to wander about aimlessly and never accomplish anything for Him or His divine purpose. As a woman, I like to have stability in my life. I like to know where I am headed. It comforts me to know that God has a distinct purpose and direction for our lives and He knows that if we are constantly uprooted, we will not thrive. We need to root our stability in Christ—nothing else.

"I will give them a heart to know me, that I am the Lord. They will be my people. I will be their God. For they will return to me with all their heart." v. 7

The sixth step toward hope is accepting that God wants to give us a new heart. This is the most important point of all. One of God's main purposes for us is to have a pure heart. We cannot have the fellowship with Him that He desires if we are living in sin. Take a moment to think back at your life. Perhaps you have wondered before what life would be like if you could have a second chance to live it over. We have all thought about that, haven't we? We would find ourselves making this sort of declaration:

"**Next time**, we wouldn't make those mistakes.

Next time, we would make better and wiser decisions.

Next time, we would live life with more passion for God."

But we can't go back and change things. You and I both know that. We can only go forward from this point in time. We need to get rid of the old heart and get a new one. Listen to these two passages of promise from Ezekiel (Jeremiah's contemporary of the day) that deal expressly with the heart.

> Ezekiel 11:19-20—*"I will give them an undivided heart and put a new spirit in them; I will remove from them their heart of stone and give them a heart of flesh. Then they will follow my decrees and be careful to keep my laws. They will be my people, and I will be their God."*

> Ezekiel 36:26-28—*"I will give you a new heart and put a new spirit in you; I will remove from you your heart of stone and give you a heart of flesh. And I will put my Spirit in you and move you to follow my decrees and be careful to keep my laws. You will live in the land I gave your forefathers; you will be my people, and I will be your God."*

God promises us right here and now that we can have a fresh start with a new heart. That's right! A fresh start with a new heart, *right now.* All we have to do is ask. He is right there waiting with a new heart for you and for me. All we have to do is make a choice.

These six points can be life changing if we will take the time to apply them to our hearts. And that's just it. Our sorrow over our past sins can be completely removed if we just take the time to deal with them properly. It is a relatively simple process. We need to ask forgiveness for the sins we've committed and we need to turn from the temptations that have taken us to these dark places. But beware! Satan doesn't want us to deal with our sinful shortcomings because, if we remain in this place of condemnation, he knows that we will never amount to anything for Christ. He is going to fight all of our attempts at restoration. He will constantly bring to mind all of our failures. Our sins that have been removed as far as the east is from the west by our loving God will be corralled like horses by Satan and paraded through our minds. To protect ourselves from his ploys, we need to seek the Lord, keep ourselves humble, and continually pray for protection and guidance.

This reminds me of one last example that I want to share with you before we conclude this chapter on past mistakes. It involves King Manasseh of Judah. He was an evil king that disregarded the ways of the Lord. He knew better. He had no excuse. He had access to all the annals of the kings that had reigned before him. If he had just taken the time to read them, he may have learned a thing or two. But instead, he chose his own way and he did what was right in his own eyes. God wasn't about to let him get away with his disobedience of worshipping other gods so God severely punished him by leading him and his people captive.

Manasseh was totally humiliated in front of his people. He had a hook put in his nose, was bound with shackles, and was taken to Babylon. He was made a public spectacle along the way. Only when he chose to humble himself, did God change His mind about Manasseh's punishment. In 2 Chronicles 33:10-13 we see this.

> [10] "*The Lord spoke to Manasseh and his people, but they paid no attention.* [11] *So the Lord brought against them the army commander of the king of Assyria, who took Manasseh prisoner, put a hook in his nose, bound him with bronze shackles and took him to Babylon (around 681 B.C.).* [12] *In his distress he sought the favor of the Lord his God and humbled himself greatly before the God of his fathers.* [13] *And when he prayed to him, the Lord was moved by his entreaty and listened to his plea; so he brought him back to Jerusalem and to his kingdom. Then Manasseh knew that the Lord is God.*"*

In this last sentence, "knew" means to ascertain by *seeing* or to *acknowledge*. Manasseh finally recognized his sins and acknowledged that he was to blame! So how did King Manasseh rectify all that he had done wrong? There are three basic steps that he took.

We see that:

1. He sought the favor of the Lord. (v. 12)

    He didn't wait for a change to come about, he made it happen. He sought or went after God on his own. He didn't wait or procrastinate.

2. He humbled himself greatly before God. (v. 12)

    He didn't just humble himself a little bit. He laid it all out before God. I imagine that he fell prostrate before him wishing that every limb could go even lower and just sink into the earth. When we are humbled greatly, we have nothing more to hide. It's all out there on the table where everyone can see. The only choice we have is to make it right and start all over again, afresh and anew.

3. And lastly, He prayed. v. 13

    He knew what he had to do. It required forgiveness from an Almighty God. He had to recognize and admit what was wrong in his life and have a change of heart toward what was right. Only a loving and forgiving God could grant his request.

But when we study how King Manasseh took these three steps toward restoration, it is interesting to see that God took three steps of His own in response to his actions. We find in verse 13 that:

*   God was **moved** by his entreaty.
*   God **listened** to his plea.
*   And, God **brought** him back.

We know that our captivity by sin, our personal "exile," can be a tough place to reside, no matter how we got there. But hope was not just given to Israel and Judah, there is hope for us today as well. We need to be honest with ourselves. Where are we today in our own personal walk with Christ? What is hindering us? Perhaps we need Christ as our own personal Savior to free us from our bondage of sin. Or, maybe we have personally committed sins that we are suffering from in our own life? Or perhaps we are the victim of others—forced to bear consequences we didn't ever want or ask for?

No matter our place in time right now, God has a way out of these burdens of bondage and captivity for us. He deeply desires good for His children. He wants joy for us, and knows that all things can work out for our good. No matter where we are, He wants us to come to Him asking forgiveness. ...He wants us to come to Him in submission and trust. ...He wants us to come humbly—recognizing His power and presence in our lives. He's ready, **right now**, to free us from our past mistakes, to grant mercy and forgiveness, and to give a fresh start with a new heart to all who will ask.

Chapter 10

Identity Protection
for the Future

"For though we live in the world, we do not wage war as the world does. The weapons we fight with are not the weapons of the world" (2 Corinthians 10:3-4a).

As we close our study on Satan's attempts to steal our personal and spiritual identities, we need to put on the final pieces of our armor that are essential in this fight against Satan. So far, we have disclosed Satan's plot against us, we have seen how hideous and formidable he really is, we have seen God's perfect plan for us, and we have found out who we really are through Christ. We have strategized about how to protect our walk with God, protect our inner and outer circles of priorities in our lives, and protect our minds from our past. We have been challenged to toss this life of fear that we live in and embrace the peace and protection that a consistent walk with Christ offers.

Are we sure we are ready to face the unknown that lurks around the corner? Are we fully equipped to handle each temptation that comes our way? God's Word tells us in 1 Corinthians 10:13 that *"No temptation has seized you except what is common to man. And God is faithful; he will not let you be tempted beyond what you can bear. But when you are tempted, he will also provide a way out so that you can stand up under it."*

According to the Bible, we can handle all of the temptations that come our way. In fact, we have even been provided with a way of escape! Many times the problem we get hung up on is that we don't like the way of escape offered by God. Perhaps it is too hurtful. Perhaps it is too painful. Perhaps it is too embarrassing. Perhaps it is uncomfortable. Perhaps it is the less popular way. Whatever the case, many times we choose to reject our escape and allow Satan to gain a foothold in our lives. We can't let him do that!

I am reminded of my children as I ponder these battles of temptation. Many times they come to me and ask if they can have something or go somewhere. I may give them the permission that they are seeking, but many times I will put a stipulation on it. Now, mind you, it is not an unreasonable stipulation. It may be something like "Clean your room" or "Do your homework for this weekend before you can do it." But sometimes when they have heard my conditions, they get their feathers ruffled and go off and sulk. They had full permission granted to them, but it was contingent on something they had to fulfill first. They did not want to expend a little effort to reap the reward they were seeking.

Aren't we just like that? God has given us a glorious identity through His Son, Jesus Christ. He has given us so many precious promises of protection and blessing for our Christian walk, but we ignore His outstretched arms. We would rather do it our own way and suffer the consequences. When we finally realize our mistake, we wish that we would have listened to Him.

God has given us plenty of warnings about what will happen in these last days. He told us our identities would be questioned. He knew what was in store for us. Have we ever taken the time to pay heed to His warnings? Well, why don't we take a look at these warnings in 2 Peter 3 by way of a little story? Drift back in time with me and imagine that it went something like this...

Peter's death was inevitable. His years of labor to expand the work that Jesus Christ had started would soon come to an end. He had fought hard for his faith during the years. More in his last years than his first, he admitted.

Since denying Jesus three times as He was tried before government officials, he had determined to give his life completely to Jesus' call to be fishers of men. Even in some of His final words Christ had said to go and make disciples of the nations—to continue the calling to be fishers of men. It was his duty to spread the Gospel and he had been given the authority he needed to accomplish the mission through the power of Jesus Christ. But he didn't have much time left.

With his martyrdom looming, he had to write one more letter. They needed to hear it again! This faith he preached was real. How could he get them to believe that! The last days were coming and people were determined to silence the voice of the Christians. Oh, they needed to beware! They needed to keep their thoughts pure and remember the words of the prophets of the past and the commands given by the Lord. Peter picked up his pen...

Dear Friends,

I want to remind you of something before I am taken through death to my eternal home. Remember, in the last days people will taunt you and ridicule you. They will try to convince you that you should follow their evil ways. They will try to discredit your faith by laughing at you. They will tell you that Christ is not real and that He is not coming back. They will say that nothing has changed from the beginning of creation, and it won't change in the days to come. But friends, you know that a day is like a thousand years to the Lord, and a thousand years is like a day. God's timing is not like man's timing. You can't base the future on the false assumptions of man. The Lord always keeps His promises. His fiery destruction of the earth as we know it is eminent. He doesn't want anyone to perish. He wants all men to come to repentance before this takes place.

But beware! The Lord will come like a thief in the night. You won't be expecting it. When that happens, the heavens will disappear and the earth will be destroyed by fire. Everything will be exposed. Since I am telling you this, you have to live holy and godly lives as you look forward to the coming of the Lord. The heaven and earth will be replaced with a new heaven and a new earth which will be our eternal home. And since we are looking toward eternity, we should make every effort to be found spotless, blameless, and at peace with God. I am not just making this up! Paul warned you of this, too. He told you that ignorant and unstable people would distort the truth of the Scriptures. Yet, even though you have heard it from Paul and from me, you have to be reminded of it over and over again.

As I close this letter, I urge you to be on your guard against these men. They will try to persuade you to their erroneous teachings and their lawless ways. Don't fall into their traps! Instead, you need to be completely committed to grow in the grace and in the knowledge of our Lord and Savior Jesus Christ.

To God be the glory,
Peter

Peter sighed as he bound up his letter and wiped his pen. He had poured out his soul to them. When would they finally believe that what he was saying was true? When would they finally realize that these people who mocked them were just pawns in Satan's hands? How could they be so easily deceived?

His mind carried him back through the decades. He had been like them once before. He had chosen to deny Christ even though he knew the truth! He didn't want to be embarrassed or inconvenienced by this faith that he had embraced. Instead of behaving as Christ had taught him, he wanted to pick and choose when and where he would stand up for what he believed in. If only they would listen to him. He had taken that course that they were on and it had led to destruction. There was only one way to live this Christian life. It was to completely surrender your body, mind, and soul to the living and true God. Peter prayed in his heart that they would listen to his pleadings one last time...

Peter's heart was heavy for these Christians, wasn't it? In 2 Peter 3, we see this story unfold in Scripture. We can see the urgency of his appeal. ...His call for us to live holy and godly lives. ...His pleading to be spotless, blameless, and at peace with God. ...His urgings to be on guard against the false teachings of the end times. How relevant this is to us today! The end times are approaching fast. The media, our government officials, our schools, our society, and even some of our churches are denying the validity of the Bible's claims. A book once held in high regard, is now touted as a bundle of fairy tales and lies. We have come so far from the truth. Sadly, many unsuspecting Christians have fallen into this trap set by Satan. Decades and decades of the media's influence have warped our morals. What we once thought was wrong has become questionable, or even considered right, by society's standards. Can't we see the stronghold that Satan has created to disarm us in these last days? I sure hope we can.

Together, we can stand up and fight for the truth. It doesn't matter if our army is small. Remember how Gideon was able to defeat the great army of the Midianites with only three hundred men in Judges 7? He had originally assembled an army of 32,000 but Judges 7:2 said that God had reduced its size *"lest Israel claim the glory for itself"* (NKJV) and *"boast...that her own strength has saved her"* (NIV).

Size doesn't matter to God. For us, we equivocate size with strength. But God thinks differently for we have been told in Romans 8:31b that, *"If God is with us, then who can be against us?"* He goes on to tell us in verses 37-39 of the same chapter that:

> *"No, in all these things we are more than conquerors through him who loved us. For I am convinced that neither death nor life, neither angels nor demons, neither the present nor the future, nor any powers, neither height nor depth, nor anything else in all creation, will be able to separate us from the love of God that is in Christ Jesus our Lord."*

Satan doesn't stand a chance against an Almighty God. And if we claim our position as conquerors through Christ, then he doesn't stand a chance against us either! We must protect ourselves from his attempts to steal our identities in Christ. Our identities belong to us, not Satan! Let's take a moment now to look at our final set of steps to protect us.

Steps to Protect

As we look at these last steps of protection, I want to take a quick detour to the hall of faith found in Hebrews 11. In particular, I want us to notice the verb phrases that were used to describe Moses in verses 24 through 29. Study this passage as you are reading and pay close attention to the verbs phrases that are mentioned.

> *"By faith Moses, when he had grown up, **refused to be known** as the son of Pharaoh's daughter. He **chose to be mistreated** along with the people of God rather than to enjoy the pleasures of sin for a short time. He **regarded***

disgrace for the sake of Christ as of greater value than the treasures of Egypt, because he was looking ahead to his reward. By faith he left Egypt, not fearing the king's anger; he persevered because he saw him who is invisible. By faith he kept the Passover and the sprinkling of blood, so that the destroyer of the firstborn would not touch the firstborn of Israel. By faith the people passed through the Red Sea as on dry land; but when the Egyptians tried to do so, they were drowned."

These phrases are incredible! They reveal the power and strength of character that Moses had developed in his life over the years. They symbolize a maturity in his walk with the Lord. They speak of the trust that he had in the Lord to deliver him from any situation. And they show the respect that he had for the holy God of Israel.

If only we would model our daily walk with the intensity of Moses' actions! If we take these principles to heart, then we will be able to withstand the pressure when we realize that a walk with Christ can be difficult and that we will have to choose to take the road less traveled. We will be able to stand strong when we are ridiculed and mistreated. So as we begin to conclude our journey in identity theft, let's make a conscious effort to remember these lessons that we have learned from Moses. He didn't care what other people thought of him. He would seek the Lord when he was confronted with opposition and find his security in Him. He was such a humble man, but God used him mightily in His plan for the children of Israel.

Our final steps of protection in this study can be found in 2 Corinthians 10. In this passage, Paul is writing to the Corinthians and is appealing to them to live boldly. Take a look at verses 3 through 7:

³"For though we live in the world, we do not wage war as the world does. ⁴The weapons we fight with are not the weapons of the world. On the contrary, they have divine power to demolish strongholds. ⁵We demolish arguments and every pretension that sets itself up against the knowledge of God, and we take captive every thought to make it obedient to Christ. ⁶And we will be ready to punish every act of disobedience, once your obedience is complete. ⁷You are looking only on the surface of things. If anyone is confident that he belongs to Christ, he should consider again that we belong to Christ just as much as he."

As you refer to each of these verses in your Bible, there are several steps that we need to list. In verse three, we see that we don't wage war the way the world does. We may live in the world, but we don't have to practice or follow its methods. Take a moment to list some ways that show how we can live differently than the world does:

_____

_____

_____

Verse four tells us the extent of the powers that we have through Jesus Christ. It says that we don't need these worldly weapons because we have the divine power to diminish strongholds! So many times we think that we are powerless to conquer our strongholds on our own. But God's Word says right here that we have been given all the power we need. Based on this study of identity theft, what are some strongholds that you need to conquer in order to keep you from becoming susceptible to Satan's attacks against you?

_____

_____

_____

In verse five, we can see that we have the power to demolish the arguments that society makes against our faith. We should also be able to see through the faulty doctrines that are contrary to the Word of God. Then we need to take our thoughts captive and force them to be in obedience to Christ. How can we personally rid ourselves of the worldly arguments and the doctrines of man and make our thoughts be pleasing to the Lord?

_____

_____

_____

_____

Verse six tells us that we should be ready to punish our disobedience. Think of the word "ready." According to the dictionary, it means "prepared mentally or physically for some experience or action; prepared for immediate use." I think of being ready as a constant awareness of the consequences of our actions. If we realize the resulting consequence from all that we do, then we are less likely to stray from what is right.

I am reminded of the saying, "Think before you speak." My mom quoted this over and over when I was a child because I had the tendency to just blurt things out without taking the time to think about what I was saying. So with warnings heeded, we practice the art of thinking first in the effort to prevent something hurtful or unkind from exiting the mouth. Take a few moments and list some of the areas that you need to be more obedient in and that Satan could be using to steal your identity:

_____

_____

_____

_____

Lastly, in verse 7, we see this final warning. *"Don't just look on the surface or outward appearance of things."* We need to live our lives with the knowledge that God looks at the heart. Our outside doesn't matter as much as our inside does. What are some things that capture your attention or focus because of their outer appearance? How do they keep you from your true identity in Christ?

_____

_____

_____

_____

It is time to start being real with ourselves. Satan is on the prowl. He loves his job of identity theft. In order to fight this continual fight against Satan, we must constantly look within. The hidden secrets of the heart need to come to light and we need to live our lives with the power that the blood of Christ has given us. We have been forgiven. We have been redeemed. But with that forgiveness and redemption comes some personal responsibility if we want to experience the full joy of God's salvation.

God wants us to be successful and happy as we walk through life with Him. He knows that Satan is out to convince us that we are nothing more than a failure. Satan want us to think that we are undeserving of anything that God could give us. He wants us to believe that we are unusable and ineffective for God. We can't let him do this to us. It's time to take our personal identities back and stop Satan's attempts at identity theft once and for all.

BIBLIOGRAPHY

Works Cited

Chapter 1

MacArthur, John. *The MacArthur Bible Commentary*. Nashville: Thomas Nelson Publishers, 2005.

Chapter 2

http://www.merriam-webster.com, accessed on October 6, 2009.

Henry, Matthew. *Matthew Henry's Commentary on the Whole Bible*. Old Tappan: Fleming H. Revell Company.

Pfeiffer, Charles and Everett F. Harrison. *The Wycliffe Bible Commentary*. Chicago: Moody Press, 1962.

MacArthur, John. *The MacArthur Bible Commentary*. Nashville: Thomas Nelson Publishers, 2005.

Todd, John. http://www.deeptruths.com; John Todd, accessed October 6, 2009.

http://wiki.answers.com, accessed October 6, 2009.

http://www.religioustolerance.org, accessed October 6, 2009.

http://www.biblegateway.com/keyword/satan.htm, accessed October 6, 2009.

http://www.markbeast.com/satan.htm, accessed October 7, 2009.

http://www.biblestudy.org/question/list-of-different-names-bible-uses-for-the-devil.htm, accessed October7, 2009.

Chapter 3

Wiersbe, Warren W. *The Bible Exposition Commentary*. Wheaton: Victor Books, 1989.

Henry, Matthew. *Matthew Henry's Commentary on the Whole Bible*. Old Tappan: Fleming H. Revell Company.

Chapter 4

Strong, James. *Abingdon's Strong's Exhaustive Concordance of the Bible.* Nashville: Abingdon Press, 1890.

Wilkinson, Bruce and Kenneth Boa. *Talk Thru The Bible.* Nashville: Thomas Nelson Publishers, 1983.

Pfeiffer, Charles and Everett F. Harrison. *The Wycliffe Bible Commentary.* Chicago: Moody Press, 1962.

Wiersbe, Warren W. *The Bible Exposition Commentary.* Wheaton: Victor Books, 1989.

MacArthur, John. *The MacArthur Bible Commentary.* Nashville: Thomas Nelson Publishers, 2005.

Chapter 5

Halley, Henry H. *Halley's Bible Handbook.* Grand Rapids: Zondervan Publishing House, 1965.

Brand, Chad, Charles Draper, and Archie England. *Holman Illustrated Bible Dictionary.* Nashville: Holman Bible Publishers, 2003.

Chapter 6

http://www.merriam-webster.com, accessed on June 15, 2011.

Strong, James. *Abingdon's Strong's Exhaustive Concordance of the Bible.* Nashville: Abingdon Press, 1890.

MacArthur, John. *The MacArthur Bible Commentary.* Nashville: Thomas Nelson Publishers, 2005.

Wiersbe, Warren W. *The Bible Exposition Commentary.* Wheaton: Victor Books, 1989.

Chapter 7

MacArthur, John. *The MacArthur Bible Commentary.* Nashville: Thomas Nelson Publishers, 2005.

Pfeiffer, Charles and Everett F. Harrison. *The Wycliffe Bible Commentary.* Chicago: Moody Press, 1962.

Joiner, Reggie. Excerpt taken from the *John Maxwell's Leadership Bible.* Thomas Nelson, 2010

http://www.merriam-webster.com, accessed on June 15, 2011.

Chapter 8

Henry, Matthew. *Matthew Henry's Commentary on the Whole Bible.* Old Tappan: Fleming H. Revell Company.

Brand, Chad, Charles Draper, and Archie England. *Holman Illustrated Bible Dictionary.* Nashville: Holman Bible Publishers, 2003.

Chapter 9

MacArthur, John. *The MacArthur Bible Commentary.* Nashville: Thomas Nelson Publishers, 2005.

Henry, Matthew. *Matthew Henry's Commentary on the Whole Bible.* Old Tappan: Fleming H. Revell Company.

Brand, Chad, Charles Draper, and Archie England. *Holman Illustrated Bible Dictionary.* Nashville: Holman Bible Publishers, 2003.

Bunyan, John. *The Pilgrim's Progress.* Grand Rapids: Baker Publishing Group, 1965.

Chapter 10

http://www.merriam-webster.com, accessed on June 17, 2011.

Appendix

http://www.markbeast.com/satan.htm, accessed October 7, 2009.

NAMES OF SATAN

(www.markbeast.com)

"The Bible calls Satan by many different names.

Abaddon - Hebrew name for Satan meaning "Destruction". "And they had as king over them the angel of the bottomless pit, whose name in Hebrew is Abaddon, but in Greek he has the name Apollyon." Revelation 9:11

Accuser - "Then I heard a loud voice saying in heaven, 'Now salvation, and strength, and the kingdom of our God, and the power of His Christ have come, for the accuser of our brethren, who accused them before our God day and night, has been cast down.'" Revelation 12:10

Adversary - "Be sober, be vigilant; because your adversary the devil walks about like a roaring lion, seeking whom he may devour." 1 Peter 5:8

Angel of light - "And no wonder! For Satan himself transforms himself into an angel of light." 2 Corinthians 11:14

Angel of the bottomless pit - "And they had as king over them the angel of the bottomless pit, whose name in Hebrew is Abaddon, but in Greek he has the name Apollyon." Revelation 9:11

Anointed covering cherub - "You were the anointed cherub who covers; I established you; You were on the holy mountain of God; You walked back and forth in the midst of fiery stones." Ezekiel 28:14

Antichrist - "And every spirit that does not confess that Jesus Christ has come in the flesh is not of God. And this is the spirit of the Antichrist, which you have heard was coming, and is now already in the world." 1 John 4:3

Apollyon - Greek name for Satan meaning "Destroyer". "And they had as king over them the angel of the bottomless pit, whose name in Hebrew is Abaddon, but in Greek he has the name Apollyon." Revelation 9:11

Beast - "⁹ Then a third angel followed them, saying with a loud voice, 'If anyone worships the beast and his image, and receives his mark on his forehead or on his hand, ¹⁰ he himself shall also drink of the wine of the wrath of God, which is poured out full strength into the cup of His indignation. He shall be tormented with fire and brimstone in the presence of the holy angels and in the presence of the Lamb.'" Revelation 14:9,10

Beelzebub - "Now when the Pharisees heard it they said, 'This fellow does not cast out demons except by Beelzebub, the ruler of the demons.'" Matthew 12:24

Belial - "And what accord has Christ with Belial? Or what part has a believer with an unbeliever?" 2 Corinthians 6:15

Deceiver - "So the great dragon was cast out, that serpent of old, called the Devil and Satan, who deceives the whole world; he was cast to the earth, and his angels were cast out with him." Revelation 12:9

Devil - "He who sins is of the devil, for the devil has sinned from the beginning. For this purpose the Son of God was manifested, that He might destroy the works of the devil." 1 John 3:8

Dragon - "So the great dragon was cast out, that serpent of old, called the Devil and Satan, who deceives the whole world; he was cast to the earth, and his angels were cast out with him." Revelation 12:9

Enemy - "The enemy who sowed them is the devil, the harvest is the end of the age, and the reapers are the angels." Matthew 13:39

Evil one - "I do not pray that You should take them out of the world, but that You should keep them from the evil one." John 17:15

Father of lies - "You are of your father the devil, and the desires of your father you want to do. He was a murderer from the beginning, and does not stand in the truth, because there is no truth in him. When he speaks a lie, he speaks from his own resources, for he is a liar and the father of it." John 8:44

God of this age - "Whose minds the god of this age has blinded, who do not believe, lest the light of the gospel of the glory of Christ, who is the image of God, should shine on them." 2 Corinthians 4:4

King of Babylon - "That you will take up this proverb against the king of Babylon, and say: 'How the oppressor has ceased, The golden city ceased!'" Isaiah 14:4

King of the bottomless pit - "And they had as king over them the angel of the bottomless pit, whose name in Hebrew is Abaddon, but in Greek he has the name Apollyon." Revelation 9:11

King of Tyre - "Son of man, take up a lamentation for the king of Tyre, and say to him, 'Thus says the Lord GOD: "You were the seal of perfection, Full of wisdom and perfect in beauty."'" Ezekiel 28:12

Lawless one - "⁸ And then the lawless one will be revealed, whom the Lord will consume with the breath of His mouth and destroy with the brightness of His coming. ⁹ The coming of the lawless one is according to the working of Satan, with all power, signs, and lying wonders, ¹⁰ and with all unrighteous deception among those who perish, because they did not receive the love of the truth, that they might be saved." 2 Thessalonians 2:8-10

Leviathan - "In that day the LORD with His severe sword, great and strong, Will punish Leviathan the fleeing serpent, Leviathan that twisted serpent; And He will slay the reptile that is in the sea." Isaiah 27:1

Liar - "You are of your father the devil, and the desires of your father you want to do. He was a murderer from the beginning, and does not stand in the truth, because there is no truth in him. When he speaks a lie, he speaks from his own resources, for he is a liar and the father of it." John 8:44

Little horn - " ⁹ And out of one of them came a little horn which grew exceedingly great toward the south, toward the east, and toward the Glorious Land. [10] And it grew up to the host of heaven; and it cast down some of the host and some of the stars to the ground, and trampled them. [11] He even exalted himself as high as the Prince of the host; and by him the daily sacrifices were taken away, and the place of His sanctuary was cast down." Daniel 8:9-11

Lucifer - "[12] How you are fallen from heaven, O Lucifer, son of the morning! How you are cut down to the ground, You who weakened the nations! [13] For you have said in your heart: 'I will ascend into heaven, I will exalt my throne above the stars of God; I will also sit on the mount of the congregation On the farthest sides of the north; [14] I will ascend above the heights of the clouds, I will be like the Most High.'" Isaiah 14:12-14

Man of sin - "[3] Let no one deceive you by any means; for that Day will not come unless the falling away comes first, and the man of sin is revealed, the son of perdition, [4] who opposes and exalts himself above all that is called God or that is worshiped, so that he sits as God in the temple of God, showing himself that he is God." 2 Thessalonians 2:3,4

Murderer - "[44] You are of your father the devil, and the desires of your father you want to do. He was a murderer from the beginning, and does not stand in the truth, because there is no truth in him. When he speaks a lie, he speaks from his own resources, for he is a liar and the father of it." John 8:44

Power of darkness - "[13] He has delivered us from the power of darkness and conveyed us into the kingdom of the Son of His love, [14] in whom we have redemption through His blood, the forgiveness of sins." Colossians 1:13, 14

Prince of the power of the air - "[1] And you He made alive, who were dead in trespasses and sins, [2] in which you once walked according to the course of this world, according to the prince of the power of the air, the spirit who now works in the sons of disobedience." Ephesians 2:1,2

Roaring lion - "Be sober, be vigilant; because your adversary the devil walks about like a roaring lion, seeking whom he may devour." 1 Peter 5:8

Rulers of the darkness - "For we do not wrestle against flesh and blood, but against principalities, against powers, against the rulers of the darkness of this age, against spiritual hosts of wickedness in the heavenly places." Ephesians 6:12

Ruler of demons - "But some of them said, 'He casts out demons by Beelzebub, the ruler of the demons.'" Luke 11:15

Ruler of this world - "³¹ Now is the judgment of this world; now the ruler of this world will be cast out. ³² And I, if I am lifted up from the earth, will draw all peoples to Myself." John 12:31,32

Satan
"And He was there in the wilderness forty days, tempted by Satan, and was with the wild beasts; and the angels ministered to Him." Mark 1:13

Serpent of old - "So the great dragon was cast out, that serpent of old, called the Devil and Satan, who deceives the whole world; he was cast to the earth, and his angels were cast out with him." Revelation 12:9

Son of perdition - "³ Let no one deceive you by any means; for that Day will not come unless the falling away comes first, and the man of sin is revealed, the son of perdition, ⁴ who opposes and exalts himself above all that is called God or that is worshiped, so that he sits as God in the temple of God, showing himself that he is God." 2 Thessalonians 2:3,4

Star - "Then the fifth angel sounded: And I saw a star fallen from heaven to the earth. To him was given the key to the bottomless pit." Revelation 9:1

Tempter - "Now when the tempter came to Him, he said, 'If You are the Son of God, command that these stones become bread.'" Matthew 4:3

Thief - "The thief does not come except to steal, and to kill, and to destroy. I have come that they may have life, and that they may have it more abundantly." John 10:10

Wicked one - "Above all, taking the shield of faith with which you will be able to quench all the fiery darts of the wicked one." Ephesians 6:16

Chapter 1: Identity Theft

*"But you are a chosen people, a royal priesthood, a holy nation,
a people belonging to God, that you may declare the praises
of Him who called you out of darkness into His wonderful light."*
1Peter 2:9

Review

In your own words, explain what "Identity Theft" means in our world today.

_____

_____

_____

Now, explain what "Identity Theft" means as it relates to our identity in Christ.

_____

_____

_____

According to 1 Peter 2:9, what does the Bible say about our identity?

_____

_____

_____

How does 2 Peter 1:3 prepare or encourage us to defend our identities against theft?

_____

_____

_____

Name some Bible characters who struggled with their identities and describe their personal battles with their identities.

_____

_____

_____

CHAPTER 2: JUST WHO DOES SATAN THINK HE IS?

"Be sober, be vigilant; because your adversary the devil walks about like a roaring lion, seeking whom he may devour."
I Peter 5:8 (NKJV)

Review

What is Webster's definition of Satan/the Devil?

_____

_____

_____

What does he look like?

_____

_____

_____

What are some of his attributes?

_____

_____

_____

What are some of the names that he is called?

_____

_____

_____

What does Satan do?

_____

_____

_____

What happens when you are under the influence of Satan? Read Luke 8: 26-35

1. You won't _____ about the things of _____.
2. You won't _____ about how your _____.
3. You won't be in _____ _____ _____.

But if you live under the power of Christ, you will:
1. _____
2. _____
3. _____

CHAPTER 3: SATAN'S PLAN TO STEAL YOUR IDENTITY

"The thief (Satan) comes only to steal and kill and destroy;
I have come that they may have life, and have it to the full." John 10:10

Review
Satan's Plan
Satan wants to change your mind about what is _____.
Satan wants to change how you live by altering the _____.
Satan wants to _____ you.
Satan wants to _____ you.
Why?_____
_____
_____
_____
_____
_____

Steps to Protect
First of all, remember the three things that Satan has purposed to do on earth:
Satan has come to _____, _____, and _____.

Second, we need to claim and apply the three principles found in
1 Peter 5:9.

1. R_____ __h_____. James 4:7

    What will happen if you do this? _____

2. S_____ f_____ ___ _____ f_____.

    (Read Eph. 6:14-17 for ways we can accomplish this.)

    v. 14 The _____ of truth buckled around your waist,
    with the _____ of righteous-
    ness in place.

    v. 15 Your feet should be fitted with _____
    that comes from the _____ of
    _____.

    v. 16 In addition to all of this, take up the _____
    of _____, with which you can extinguish all the
    _____ _____ of the devil or evil one.

    v. 17 Take the_____ of_____
    and the _____ of the _____,
    which is the word of God.

3. Remember, you are not alone.

CHAPTER 4: GOD'S PERFECT PLAN FOR US

"For I desire mercy, not sacrifice, and acknowledgment of God rather than burnt offerings." Hosea 6:6

Review

God's Plan for Us

God wants us to do "great" things for Him. Some of these "great" things are found in the following principles.

1. The greatest among you shall be like a little _____.
   Matt. 18:1-7

2. In order to be great (or exalted), we must be _____.
   Matt. 23:11-12

3. We must be like a _____ if we want to be great.
   Luke 22:25-30

4. The greatest thing that we can do as Christians is to _____.
   1 Cor. 13:13

5. There's no greater commandment than to love _____ and our _____. Mark 12:28-34

6. Another great thing that we must do is _____ _____ _____ _____.
   Matt. 28:19-20

7. If we follow God's Word, we will have great _____. Ps. 19:7-11

As we ponder the story of Ezra, we see that His faithfulness _____ God resulted in a return of faithfulness _____ God.

Steps to Protect

1. Prepare ourselves by building a firm _____
    on the _____ of _____. We need to _____
    God's Word into _____. Luke 6:46-49, Phil. 4:9

2. Equip ourselves with _____ _____ for
    doing His Will. Hebrews 13:21, 2 Timothy 3:16-17

3. Be guided by the _____ ____ _____.
    Ps. 119:105

Write down what you believe is God's specific plan for your life.

_____

_____

_____

_____

_____

_____

CHAPTER 5: WHO AM I?

*"For we are God's workmanship, created in Christ Jesus to do good works,
which God has prepared in advance for us to do."* Ephesians 2:10

Review
Who Am I?

1. We are His _____. Eph. 2:10

2. We are made in the _____ ___ _____. Col. 3:10, 11

3. We are called to be _____ ___ _____. Eph 5:1

4. We are _____ _____ ___ _____. Eph. 2:13

5. We are the _____ ____ _____ _____. Matt. 5:14

6. We are His _____, yet we are _____.
   1 Peter 2:16, 1 Cor. 4:1

7. We are a new_____. 2 Cor. 5:17, Eph. 4:22-24

8. We are His _____which makes us His _____.

   Gal. 3:26, 29; Rom. 8:17; Titus 3:7

9. We are _____to be _____. Col. 1:24-29

10. We are _____. 1 Pet. 2:9

Steps to Protect

Remember:

1. If I am His workmanship, then I can do whatever He

   _____.

2. If I am made in His image, then I shouldn't complain about

   _____.

3. If I am an imitator of God, then I can _____

   _____.

4. If I have been brought near to God, then I can
   _____ whenever I need to.

5. If I am the light of the world, then I can _____

   _____.

6. If I am His servant, then I will

   _____ for Him.

7. If I am free, then I can live my life without _____

   _____.

8. If I am a new creation, then I have _____

   _____.

9. If I am His child, then He _____

   _____.

10. If I am His heir, then I will _____

    _____.

11. If I am chosen, then I _____

CHAPTER 6: PROTECTING MY WALK WITH GOD

*"He has showed you, O man, what is good, and what does the
Lord require of you?
"To act justly and to love mercy and to walk humbly with your God."*
Micah 6:8

Review
My Walk with God

Daniel 10 gives us insight into three steps in his walk with God.

1. He was _____.

2. He set his mind to _____ _____.

3. He _____ himself before God.

Steps to Protect

To protect myself from Satan's grasp, I need to strengthen my walk with God in these specific areas found in Colossians 3:1-17:

Verse	Action
v. 1-4	
v. 5-6	
v. 7-9	
v. 10-11	
v. 12	

v. 13 _____
_____

v. 14 _____
_____

v. 15 _____
_____

v. 16 _____
_____

v. 17 _____
_____

For further study: Ecclesiastes 12:13; Joshua 1:7-9; Deuteronomy 4:9, 6:5-9, 8:6, and 10:12-13; Ephesians 3,4, and 5; Galatians 5; and 1 Peter 1, 4.

Chapter 7: Protecting My Family Priorities

"The wise woman builds her house, but with her own hands the foolish one tears hers down." Proverbs 14:1

Review
My Family Priorities

There are three attitudes that wives can have. List each type and the conflicts or benefits that result from each attitude.

1. The "_____" Wife -- _____
   _____
   _____

2. The "_____" Wife -- _____
   _____
   _____

3. The "_____" Wife -- _____
   _____
   _____

There are three types of parenting styles that can be acquired. List each type and the conflicts or benefits that result from each style.

1. "_____" Parenting -- _____
   _____
   _____

2. "_____" Parenting -- _____
   _____
   _____

3. "_____" Parenting -- _____
   _____
   _____

List out the priorities that single women face and some of the conflicts or benefits that are encountered. _____
_____
_____

Steps to Protect

Read Proverbs 14:1 and list out the two choices that we can make as women. What does the wise woman choose to do?
_____
_____
_____

Chapter 8: Protecting My Career and Calling

"Therefore, my dear brothers, stand firm. Let nothing move you.
Always give yourselves fully to the work of the Lord,
because you know that your labor in the Lord is not in vain."
1 Corinthians 15:58

Review
My Career and Calling

Our career, or work, should go hand in hand with our _____.

What can we learn from Lydia's example in Acts 16? List the six basic areas that we can apply to our own lives.

1. _____
   _____

2. _____
   _____

3. _____
   _____

4. _____
   _____

5. _____
   _____

6. _____
   _____

Steps to Protect

There are five steps that we can take to protect our career and calling. Write down these five areas that help in our fight against Satan.

W – _____
_____

O – _____
_____

R – _____
_____

L – _____
_____

D – _____
_____

CHAPTER 9: PROTECTING MY MIND FROM THE PAST

"Forget the former things; do not dwell on the past."
Isaiah 43:18

Review
My Past Mistakes

As we look at Jeremiah 24:5-8, we see that God gives six steps of hope that we can claim as we deal with past mistakes. Fill in the blanks from this passage of Scripture and from Chapter 9 to find these six steps.

1. I am _____ of God's salvation. (v. 5)

2. God is _____ over me. (v. 6)

3. God will _____ _____ _____ from this place I find myself in. (v. 6)

4. God's plan is to _____ _____ _____! (v. 6)

5. God wants to give me _____. (v. 6)

6. God wants to give us a _____ _____. (v. 7)

Steps to Protect

When King Manasseh finally realized his sin, he took three basic steps in order to make things right with God. Look at 2 Chronicles 33:10-13. What were they?

1. He _____ the favor of the Lord. v. 12

2. He _____ _____ greatly before God. v. 12

3. And lastly, He _____. v. 13

We see that when King Manasseh took these three basic steps, God took three of His own in 2 Chronicles 33:13. What were God's three steps?

1. He was _____ by his entreaty.

2. He _____ to his plea.

3. And, He _____ him back.

Chapter 10: Identity Protection for the Future

"For though we live in the world, we do not wage war as the world does. The weapons we fight with are not the weapons of the world."
2 Corinthians 10:3-4a

Review
Identity Protection

2 Peter 3, the Apostle Peter appeals to Christians to live holy and godly lives in the last days. After reading this chapter, what are some specific areas that we need to focus on as we live our lives for Christ?

_____

_____

_____

_____

What kind of changes will you have to make in order to obey what the Holy Spirit is telling you to do?

_____

Steps to Protect

In this last chapter, we looked at a passage about Moses in the Hall of Faith found in Hebrews 11:24-29. By looking at all the verb phrases used to describe Moses' faith, we see that Moses actively lived out his faith. What are some "verb phrases" that you would want people to use about you when they describe your personal faith?

_____

Since completing this study on Identity Theft, how will your views be strengthened as you live each day protecting your identity in Christ? What will you be more aware of? What will you do to make a difference in your life for Christ?

_____